The Best of

YOU CAN

U

with

beakmaN & jax

A Collection of the Grossest, Weirdest, Coolest Experiments *You Can* Do

jok church

Andrews McMeel
Publishing

Kansas City

mc²

www.beakman.com
www.uexpress.com
www.andrewsmcmeel.com

Library of Congress Cataloging-in-Publication Data

Church, Jok.
    The best of you can with Beakman & Jax : a collection of the grossest, weirdest, coolest experiments you can do / Jok Church.
        p.   cm.
    Summary: Includes experiments and explanations that answer questions about a variety of scientific and everyday topics, including acid rain and stomach acid, cameras and blinking, odors and perfume, and more.
    ISBN 0-8362-3666-1 (pbk.)
    1. Science—Experiments—Juvenile literature. 2. Science—Miscellanea—Juvenile literature. [1. Science—Experiments. 2. Experiments. 3. Science—Miscellanea.]   I. Title.
Q164.C444   1997   97-28519
507'.8—dc21   CIP

Note to Parents: *The Best of* You Can *with Beakman & Jax* is intended to be educational and informative. It contains relatively simple science experiments designed to interest children. Many of the experiments require adult supervision. We strongly recommend that before you allow children to conduct any of the experiments in this book that you read the experiment in its entirety and make your own determination as to the safest way of conducting the experiment.

Attention Schools and Businesses

Andrews McMeel books are available at quantity discounts with bulk purchase for educational, business, or sales promotional use. For information, please write to: Special Sales Department, Andrews McMeel Publishing, 4520 Main Street, Kansas City, Missouri 64111.

Contents

The Grossest, Weirdest, Coolest Stuff You Can Do

Acknowledgments/ Greetings

Much thanks to Lisa Tarry of Universal Press Syndicate and Stephanie Bennett, Dorothy O'Brien, and Chris Schillig of Andrews McMeel Publishing.

Generous loving assistance and support provided by: Glenn Corey, Marsha Fine, Robert Boccabella, Earl and Flo Mills, Roy and Evelyn Hoffman, Les Haber, George Ann Muntin, Paul Schwartz, Ron Pigram, Brian Runnheim, Lee Glaize, and Vicki Chase, R.N.

Something way important about this book is that you actually do the experiments with someone in your family. It helps you learn and teach each other about the question. You also get to learn a lot about each other as a bonus. I think they call that *quality time* - which also used to be called *fun*.

Doing this stuff together builds your power. You'll understand stuff and you'll be able to explain stuff to other people. You'll also open yourself up to asking a lot more questions. I think that if people would teach stuff to each other more often, this would be a much better planet.

I know that some people say the family has changed or that lots of kids don't have a real family. I think that's a big lie. We all have real families. They are the families we are born into or the kind of family we choose to be in. All kinds of families are real.

People who are growing together by their own choice are a family. And doing stuff together can help you grow together and know each other better - no matter what kind of real family you have.

Remember to keep asking questions.
Questions are the one of the most powerful things there are.

Jok Church

For my family:
Adam, Chloe,
Erin, Norn, Shannon

Other Andrews McMeel books by the author:

You Can with Beakman: Science Stuff *You Can* Do	ISBN 0-8362-7004-5
You Can with Beakman & Jax: More Science Stuff *You Can* Do	ISBN 0-8362-7008-8
You Can with Beakman & Jax: Way More Science Stuff *You Can* Do	ISBN 0-8362-7043-6
Beakman & Jax's Microscope Book (with a real microscope)	ISBN 0-8362-7021-5
Beakman & Jax's Bubble Book: Plus Everything You Need To Make Real Square Bubbles	ISBN 0-8362-2706-9

Dear Reader,

⚠ Please look for this special caution sign throughout the book. When you see this sign, it means that you need to ask a grown-up for help.

This is a book for families to use together so the grown-ups in your families should be happy to work with you.

Show your family this page.

Remember, look for this sign. It is very important. ⚠

Beakman

Beakman Place

Jax Place

Jax Place

Dear Beakman,

Why do pictures look so much better in my View-Master?

**Kadi Kiiss
San Rafael,
California**

Dear Kadi,

Most pictures are just tall and wide. Pictures in your View-Master are tall, wide and deep. Depth is the 3rd Dimension. That's where the word 3-D comes from. Here are two experiments *You Can* do to learn how 3-D works.

Beakman

Beakman Place

Seeing the Two Different Pictures

WHAT YOU NEED: Just a pencil

WHAT TO DO: Hold the pencil about 18 inches from your face and look at a window on the other side of the room. Focus on the pencil and notice the window. Now focus on the window and notice the pencil.

WHAT IS GOING ON:

When you looked at the pencil you saw 2 windows behind it. When you looked at the window you saw 2 pencils in front of it. There is really only 1 pencil and 1 window. What you are really seeing is 2 different pictures; 1 for each eye. Try the experiment again with only 1 eye open. You'll see just 1 window and 1 pencil. People who have only 1 eye that works cannot see depth. They cannot see in 3-D.

This Book Is Getting Deep

WHAT YOU NEED: This book.

WHAT TO DO: Hold the book about 12 inches from your face and look at the trees on the next page. Now cross your eyes so you can see 3 images instead of 2. Pay attention to the picture in the middle. The trick is to focus your eyes while they are crossed. It may take some time. *You Can* do it. Relax and be patient.

WHAT IS GOING ON:

You Can see the tree nearest you and the one that is far away. The two pictures are not the same. When your brain puts them together, you get 3-D. Do not look too long. Crossing your eyes can give you a headache.

The World Is Already in 3-D

We use the 3rd dimension - depth - to tell how far away things are. Humans and other animals need to do that, which is why we have 2 eyes. Each eye sees a slightly different picture.

When our brain puts those two pictures together, we get a 3-D image.

Your View-Master does the same thing. Each eye piece shows you a slightly different picture. Your brain puts them together and you see in 3-D.

Each eye sees its own picture. The brain puts them together.

9

Dear Beakman,

How can rain be acid rain?

Carolynne Good
Stratford,
Ontario

Dear Carolynne,

That's a question more and more Canadians are asking the United States. More and more rain in Eastern Canada is acidic. Air pollution in the United States seems to be the reason why.

It's happening in the U.S.A., too. Rain as acidic as lemon juice fell in Wheeling, West Virginia, and many lakes in New York State are dying from acid rain. Also there's acid rain in Germany's Black Forest.

Acid rain starts out as regular rain. But when it falls through clouds of air pollution, rain changes into a weak acid. This acid is strong enough to kill trees, dissolve marble and kill whole lakes.

Beakman
Beakman Place

Make an Acid Tester

WHAT YOU NEED:
Red cabbage - saucepan - grater -
water - help and permission from an adult

WHAT TO DO: Finely grate the red cabbage
till you have 2 cups. Just cover with water and
bring to a boil. Do not use an aluminum pan! ⚠ *Never use
the stove without permission from your family.* Simmer
for 15 minutes. Let it cool, then strain and save the liquid.

WHAT IS GOING ON: I know it's like cabbage tea and that
seems a bit disgusting. But cabbage tea is also an *indicator*. That
means if you add acid to your acid tester, it will change color.
Test different things. Add 1 teaspoon of vinegar to 1 teaspoon
of cabbage tea. What happens? It changes color to light pink.
Do the same test with a pinch of baking soda, and the juice
turns blue. Do your tests in a small clear glass so you can hold
it up to light.

Your acid tester will change from pink for acids to green
for alkalines (AL-ka-linz) - which is the opposite of acids. Things
that aren't acid or alkaline are called neutral (NEW-trahl) and are
right in the middle.

Testing Rainwater

WHAT YOU NEED: Your acid tester cabbage tea

WHAT TO DO: Test other things with your acid tester, like soap or lemon juice. You'll see what's acidic and what's alkaline. Now start collecting rainwater samples in very clean jars that you've rinsed out extra especially well. Label and date the jars.

Mix equal amounts of your acid tester with your samples of rainwater. Make notes on any color changes. It should stay the same. If the color starts moving to the reds and pinks, you may be getting acid rain.

pinks	reds	purple	blues	greens
Acid		Neutral		Alkaline

Take your rain samples to school. Your teacher can use another acid tester that's more accurate. It's called litmus paper. If your class finds any acid rain, you might want to write a class letter to your representative in Congress or Parliament.

P.S. from Jax: Acid rain is not new. It was first discovered in England in 1872. Smoke from coal was the cause. Coal and oil smoke are still the problem, 125 years later.

Dear Jason,

Your stomach does have acid inside of it - hydrochloric acid - strong enough to eat through a piece of the metal zinc.

The reason your stomach isn't destroyed by the acid is our old friend snot, which is also called mucus.

Mucus is thick, sticky, slimy and gooey. And it's a good thing. The inside of your stomach is covered with it. That layer of snot protects the stomach from its own acid. In fact, the miracle of mucus protects many parts of our bodies - some parts that even I will not mention here.

Jax Place
Jax Place

Make Some Fake Snot

WHAT YOU NEED: Light corn syrup - unflavored gelatin - measuring cup - water - family permission - microwave oven or stove

WHAT TO DO: Heat ½ cup water just until it boils. Remove heat. Sprinkle in 3 envelopes of unflavored gelatin. Let it soften a few minutes and stir with a fork. Add enough corn syrup to make 1 cup of thick glop. Stir with the fork and lift out the long strands of gunk.

SO WHAT: Mucus is made mostly out of sugars and protein. That's what you used to make your fake snot, only you used different proteins and different sugars. Did you see those long, fine strings inside your fake snot when you lifted out the fork? Those strands are proteins. They're why real snot can be stretched out real long. The protein helps make it sticky, too. Real mucus sticks to the inside of your stomach. Without it, you'd digest yourself. Real mucus has other jobs, which *You Can* learn in Experiment #2.

Now Make Some Fake Boogers

WHAT YOU NEED: Your fake snot from Experiment #1 - vacuum cleaner

WHAT TO DO: Ask someone who knows to show you the right way to change the vacuum cleaner bag. (*You Can* sell everyone on the idea of doing this experiment because you'll now *be able to help out around the house*.) Go outside with the dirt bag and your fake snot. Blow a bit of the dust from the vacuum cleaner. It's very fine and is a bad thing to breathe into our bodies. Dump a pinch of the finest dust onto your fake snot. Now stir it up. Look closely into the goo from the side. You just made fake boogers!

SO WHAT: The fine dust got trapped and suspended in the thick fake snot. That's the idea of having mucus in your nose. We use it to trap all the dust, pollen and junk that's floating in the air. Sometimes when you blow your nose, out comes gross black stuff. It's usually mucus with trapped dust. It's healthier to keep that kind of dirt outside of our bodies. And with the miracle of snot on guard, most of the schmutz is trapped and then blown out in boogers.

P.S. from Beakman: Be sure to keep this recipe in mind for Halloween. *You Can* never have too much thick, gooey, sticky, slimy stuff at Halloween.

15

How do mirrored sunglasses work?

Ben Williams
Douglasville,
Georgia

Dear Ben,

The mirrors in sunglasses are special. First, they look way cool. Second, they are *not* made out of one-way glass because there is no such thing as one-way glass.

Sunglass mirrors are called *partially silvered* mirrors. (The metal on mirrors isn't really silver anymore, but the name *silver* stuck.)

Partially silvered mirrors are coated with a thinner layer of metal than regular mirrors. That lets some of the light waves shine right through.

Jax Place
Jax Place

One-Way or Two-Way?

WHAT YOU NEED: Mirrored sunglasses - flashlight - dark room or closet

WHAT TO DO: In the light look at the front of the glasses and notice the mirror.

Go into the closet or dark room and aim the flashlight's light from inside the glasses shining outward, like in the drawing. Then try shining it from the outside inward.

SO WHAT: You just proved that light can go the wrong way through so-called *one-way* glass. Light can shine through mirrored sunglasses both ways - same with a one-way window, too. The side that looks like mirrors will look mirrored only when there is brighter light on the mirrored side. If you turn lights on behind a so-called one-way window, you can see into that room.

How to Split a Light Beam

WHAT TO DO: Set the sunglasses on the floor in the dark. Shine the light into the lens at a 45-degree angle. Put your hand or a piece of paper at the spot marked 1 and then 2. Compare the light in the two spots.

SO WHAT: About half the light is bouncing off the thin layer of metal. The rest of the light shines through it. Bouncing half the sunlight away from your eyes means less light is getting through. That protects your eyes. With only half the light getting in, the world looks a little darker. That's what sunglasses are supposed to do and is why this very, very thin metal layer works as sunglasses.

1

2

You just built something called a beam-splitter!

P.S. from Beakman: Insect screen or even a sheer drape will work like so-called one-way glass. If you're on the darker side, the screen or drape will seem to disappear.

Dear Jax,

Why does a rubber ball bounce?

**Tianna Nelson
Castro Valley,
California**

Dear Tianna,

When you drop a ball and the ball falls to the ground, the energy of the fall actually collapses the bottom of the ball.

When the ball reshapes itself, that falling energy is changed into lifting energy.

After you do this experiment, *You Can* read the reason it works by holding page 21 up to a mirror.

Jax Place

The Way the Ball Bounces

WHAT YOU NEED: Basketball - tennis ball
Optional: Any other 2 balls that are about the same sizes -
1 very big and 1 quite small. They both should bounce.

WHAT TO DO: Put a ball in each of your hands. Gently turn your hands over at the same time. Let the balls fall to the ground. Do not add any energy by pushing or throwing them down.

MORE STUFF TO DO: Now place the tennis ball on top of the basketball. Let them drop together. Again, do not add any energy by throwing the balls down to the ground.

SO WHAT: The balls bounced at about the same height during the first part of your experiment. But when you did the second part, the tennis ball zoomed off and jumped as high as a house. Why?

What Is Going On

When you bounced the balls separately, they both popped back up about the same height. And that's important if you think about it. The basketball is much bigger and is a lot heavier than the tennis ball. That means a lot more energy is needed to lift that ball up in its bounce. The tennis ball takes less energy to lift in its bounce. When you put the two together, some of the lifting energy is transferred from the basketball to the tennis ball. It was so much, the tennis ball shot off like a rocket.

P.S. from Beakman: Try it with the basketball on top of the tennis ball. Use what you just learned to figure out why it loses almost all its bounce.

Dear Jax,

Why is the color black hot?

**Melanie Stevenson
Dearborn, Michigan**

Dear Melanie,

Back in olden times in the 1960s, earth tones were hot. Now the hot colors are black, green and purple. Black is hot because it can make you look artistic and all groovy, especially black turtlenecks.

But I think you might be asking about *another* kind of hot - the temperature kind of hot.

Black things get hotter in sunlight because all colors turn into heat. Black gets hotter because it absorbs the most colors.

Jax Place
Jax Place

Make Some Rainbows

WHAT YOU NEED: Prism - sunshine
Optional: shallow pan - mirror - water

WHAT TO DO: Use either of the drawings as a guide and make your own rainbow. If you use the water method, be sure to let the water get very still and to tilt the mirror slowly until you see colors.

WHAT IS GOING ON: What looks like white light is really all colors of light mixed together. We see colors because colored light bounces off things. *When we see something, we do not see the thing. We see light bouncing off the thing!*

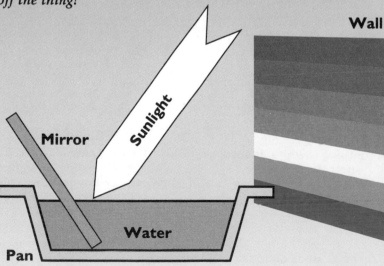

Wall

Sunlight

Mirror

Water

Pan

How Colors Bounce

If something is yellow, it absorbs all colors of light except for yellow. It reflects, or bounces back, yellow light.

If something is blue, it absorbs all colors of light except for blue. It reflects, or bounces back, blue light.

Since all colors are reflected, no colors are absorbed and no heat is produced.

If something is red, it absorbs all colors of light except for red. It reflects, or bounces back, red light.

No colors are reflected. All colors are absorbed and converted into heat.

If something is white, it absorbs no colors of light. It reflects, or bounces back, all the colors of light.

If something is black, it absorbs all colors of light. It reflects, or bounces, no colors. All the absorbed colors turn into heat.

P.S. from Beakman: If no light is bouncing off something, then there isn't any color. That means there is no color at all in darkness.

24

Dear Bill,

The best way to learn about cameras is to build one big enough to put your head inside. That way *You Can* take a look around and see what's going on. Really.

Beakman
Beakman Place

First, a Little History

World's first photograph

More than 150 years ago, in 1824, a man in the nation of France took this picture. His name was Joseph Niépce. The picture is hard to see. It was taken from an attic window and is a photo of the roof across the yard. Several other rooftops can be seen. The important thing about this picture is that it was the first time anyone was able to get a photo to last. Before this picture, photographs were experimental and they kept disappearing. The invention was not a mega hit. Niépce died flat broke. He spent all of his money on his experiments.

Get Inside a Camera

WHAT YOU NEED: Large cardboard box (make sure it can close) - masking tape - aluminum foil - nail - white paper - large bath towel

WHAT TO DO: Find the big box at a supermarket. Tell the people at the market that you need the empty box for science. They will think that's a good idea and say yes. Tape the white paper inside like in the drawing. Cut a 1-inch by 1-inch hole in the opposite side of the box and tape a piece of foil over it. Use the nail to punch a hole in the foil. Close the box and tape it all up. Tape down foil to seal the cracks. It is very important that no light at all get in the box - except through the little hole in the foil. Seal all corners and cracks. The darker the box is, the better this experiment works!

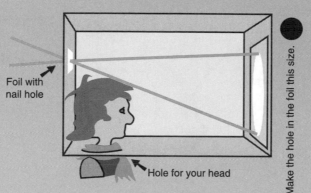

Foil with
nail hole

Make the hole in the foil this size.

Hole for your head

MORE STUFF TO DO: Look at the drawing and notice where the hole for your head is. Cut one in your box. Peek inside to see if there are light leaks. Seal them up. Take your box outside and wrap a big towel around your neck. This will keep out light. Now put the box over your head and look at the white paper. Move around and point the back of the box in different directions. You should have quite a show inside. If there are friends with you, ask them to move around. Give them a turn inside the box. The whole thing is too radical to keep for yourself.

WHAT IS GOING ON: You just made a kind of camera. It is called a camera obscura (ob-SKYUR-ah). The images you saw on the paper were upside down. That's how it is in all cameras. In a photographic camera, the white paper would be a piece of film that changes its chemistry when light hits it. In a video camera the white paper would be a device called a CCD - which stands for Charged Coupled Device. It turns light into an electrical signal. The nail hole in the foil is the lens. If

you had a friend cover it with his or her finger, that would be the shutter. Shutter speed is a way to change how long it is open. The speed of film is an ASA or ISO number. It tells how fast the film reacts to light. The lower the number, the more light you need. The f-stop changes how big the hole behind the lens is. The higher the f-stop number, the smaller the hole.

A movie camera takes 24 different pictures every second. Thomas Edison figured out the best way to move the film that fast. He punched holes on the edge of the film. They are called sprocket holes.

Dear Beakman,

Why do armpits smell?

**Dana Orr
Kingston, Ontario**

Dear Dana,

There's all kinds of stuff living on us. We're all like walking bacteria gardens and fungus farms.

Bacteria living on your skin eat skin oils and stuff in our sweat. The waste those bacteria make is what smells.

There are lots and lots of sweat glands in the palms of hands, on the soles of feet and under our arms.

When you reach age 11 to 13, lots of things get turned on - like those sweat glands. That's just the thing the bacteria need to chow down and gross you out.

Beakman

Beakman Place

Do This in School

WHAT YOU NEED: Quart jar with lid - cotton swab - sweaty friend - 4 envelopes unflavored gelatin - boiling water - teacher's help

WHAT TO DO:

Ask your teacher or another grown-up to prepare a strong mixture of gelatin with just 1 cup water and all the gelatin. Pour it into the jar; close the lid and lay it on its side to cool *completely*. You might want to make more than 1 jar so more people in the class can participate.

Even cute European guys can stink. Anybody can.

29

MORE STUFF: After recess, collect samples of bacteria from sweaty friends. Use the cotton swabs to collect it from their feet or under their arms. Gently wipe the swab in long lines on the gelatin.

Close the jar; wrap it up in a towel and keep it in a warm (not hot), dark place for 4 days. The closet will do just fine. When you open the jar, the smell will gross you out! You might even gag.

Make sure you use lots of hot water to dissolve the gelatin and pour this awful mess down the drain.

A hardworking adult can sweat as much as 4 gallons a day. Even a desk-jockey sweats about 2 quarts a day. Most sweat evaporates before you notice it.

SWEAT

SWEAT

SWEAT
1 GALLON

SWEAT
1 GALLON

Mirror Message:
Deodorants work by killing the bacteria. Antiperspirants work by interfering with your sweat glands.

P.S. from Jax: When you collect bacteria, try getting samples from places around the school—like the drinking fountain. You'll probably find bacteria there. You'll probably find it everywhere.

30

Dear Beakman,

How do the bar codes at the grocery store work?

Justin Child
Placerville,
California

Dear Justin,

If you're a cash register, the center of the universe is Dayton, Ohio - the home of a cloister called the Uniform Code Council.

Like a group of dutiful business monks, the people at the UCC are dedicated to spreading their vision of the Universal Product Code. (Anything being *universal* is a very heavy concept. Look it up.)

The UCC's UPC bar codes are read by laser beams. But *humans* with lots of patience *can* translate them, too. Keep in mind that machines can do this entire experiment in less than 1 second.

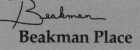

Beakman Place

Decode the Bar Code

WHAT YOU NEED: Paper and pencil - this book - patience

WHAT TO DO: There are 12 digits in a UPC. Each digit is separated into 7 tiny slices. Read the 12 digits by reading the slices. If a slice is black, write down a 1. If it's white, write down a 0. Do this for all 12. To get the UPC, match your list of 1's and 0's to the Code Key. See if you get the 12 correct UPC digits by reading the upside-down line in a mirror.

Code Key

Digit Value	Left Binary Code	Right Binary Code
0	0001101	1110010
1	0011001	1100110
2	0010011	1101100
3	0111101	1000010
4	0100011	1011100
5	0110001	1001110
6	0101111	1010000
7	0111011	1000100
8	0110111	1001000
9	0001011	1110100

On the left-hand side of the center code, use the left codes. Switch to the right codes on the right side of the center code. This mirror-image coding lets the scanner read the numbers in either direction.

Mirror Message
P.S. from Jax:
The UPC number is 0-34000-31200-0. The manufacturer's code is 34000. It is for the Hershey's company. The product code is for a medium-sized can of Hershey's chocolate syrup.

Know the Code

Start Code

Center Code

Start Code

0 12345 67890 5

The UCC proclaims these to be "human readable numbers."

The first 6 digits are a particular manufacturer's code. Every product they make will begin with these same 6 digits. This number is handed down by the UCC.

The 5-digit item number is given to the product by the company that makes it. That gives them 99,999 things they can make.

This is a *check digit*. It's the answer to a math problem designed to be sure the scanner read the right code number.

Amaze your friends! Fool the teacher! *You Can* always guess the last number of a UPC code. Use the "human readable numbers" from any 12-digit UPC code: Add the sum of the odd-spaced digits (the 1st, 3rd, 5th, 7th, 9th). Multiply the sum by 3. Save that as answer #1. Add up the even-spaced digits of the code (Don't include the check digit! That's the one you're guessing). Add that answer to answer #1. The check digit will be whatever number you have to add to your last answer to get it up to the next multiple of 10.

Right Start Code (101)

12

11

10

9

8

7

Center Code (01010)

6

5

4

3

2

1

Start here

Left Start Code (101)

Dear Charlie,

It isn't just speed that lifts a heavy airplane up in the sky. It is something called air pressure. *You Can* do these experiments to see how air pressure can push a big jet up into the sky.

Beakman
Beakman Place

WHAT YOU NEED: A clean plastic bottle - your lungs

WHAT TO DO: Look at the sides of the bottle. Then, with your mouth suck some of the air out of the bottle. What happened? Why do you think it happened?

WHAT IS GOING ON:
When you took air out of the bottle you lowered the air pressure inside it. The air pressure outside the bottle is greater, so it pushed the sides of the bottle in. Any time air pressure is not the same, the higher air pressure will push toward the lower air pressure. It is trying to make the air pressure balanced, or the same. It is the air OUTSIDE of the bottle that pushed in the sides!

WHAT YOU NEED: 2 big books - a piece of paper

WHAT TO DO: Put the big books 4 inches apart and lay the paper on top. Stoop down so you are even with the table and try blowing UNDER the paper to lift the paper up. Blow hard! What happened?

WHAT IS GOING ON:
When you blew under the paper you lowered the air pressure in the little space between the books. The higher air pressure on top of the paper pushed it down - not up like we think it would.

WHAT YOU NEED: A piece of paper - tape - scissors - pencil - canister vacuum cleaner (a kind of vacuum)

EXPERIMENT #3

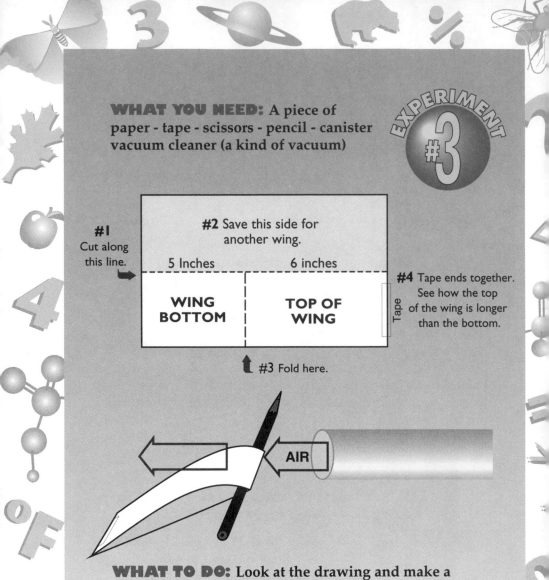

#1 Cut along this line. ➡️

#2 Save this side for another wing.

5 Inches — 6 inches

WING BOTTOM | **TOP OF WING**

Tape

#4 Tape ends together. See how the top of the wing is longer than the bottom.

⬆️ **#3** Fold here.

AIR

WHAT TO DO: Look at the drawing and make a wing. Hold it with the pencil against the back of your vacuum cleaner - the end where the air blows out. Move it up until the air is blowing over the TOP of your wing. What happened?

WHAT IS GOING ON:

When you blew air over the top of the wing, you lowered the air pressure. The air pressure on the bottom of the wing is greater, so it pushed the wing UP. Air pressure pushing up from the bottom of the wing is what keeps airplanes up in the air.

Dear Sarah,

That's a subject lots of people are really interested in. Vomit and other colorful bodily functions pull in tons of mail to my TV show. Perhaps we can answer this rather delicate question here.

Vomit is a lot like digestion in reverse – or going backward. It's a way for the body to protect itself, and no one likes it at all.

Sometimes we throw up just because our brains are getting too many different signals and can't sort them out. That's being *nauseous* (NAW-shus), which is a very popular word in junior and senior high schools.

Beakman

Beakman Place

Football and Throwing Up

WHAT YOU NEED: The big game on TV
- an imagination

WHAT TO DO: Fortunately for experimenters, there is always a football game on somewhere. Pay attention to the audience in the stadium. Sometimes you'll see everyone stand up and sit back down again so that it looks like a huge wave is rolling through the stadium. *You Can* give a report to your class on throwing up and have the class do the wave. It's a very important part of hurling chunks.

SO WHAT: The football stadium wave is a lot like a wave the muscles in your esophagus make. Your esophagus (ee-SOF-ag-gus) is a muscular tube from your mouth to your stomach. The muscles ripple down toward your stomach, behaving a lot like the stadium wave. This takes chewed food to your stomach. It's called a systolic (sis-TOL-ick) wave. When we get sick sometimes the wave reverses itself and brings up chewed food. No one likes it when that happens.

The Technicolor Yawn

Here's a vomit play-by-play:

1 You grind up food in your mouth. You also add saliva (spit), which starts digestion and also helps turn your food into a mushy paste. You swallow.

2 The muscles in the tube to your stomach work like a toothpaste tube. They squeeze the food paste down into your stomach.

3 Your stomach adds acid to the food paste to break it down into a disgusting mess.

4 The vomit center in your brain gets too many signals - you have the flu, are carsick, or maybe the food is bad and your body wants to get rid of it.

5 The sphincter (SFINK-tur) is like a door. It slams closed.

6 Your stomach squeezes in a kind of convulsion - major twitch.

7 The only place for the food paste to go is back up the tube to your mouth.

8 By now you feel awful. If there's time, you find a toilet nearby. That's why vomiting is sometimes called talking on the big white phone.

Mouth

Esophagus

Sphincter

Stomach

P.S. from Jax: You may have noticed that throwing up makes your throat burn. That's from the acid your stomach uses to dissolve food. Your stomach is protected from the acid by a coating of mucus that keeps the stomach from digesting itself.

Dear Beakman,

How does a sundial work? Is it magic?

**Daniel Dunn
London, Ontario**

Dear Daniel,

Sundials keep a *kind of time* really well. In fact, they can do it better than the finest quartz clock.

Here's a different idea about time: The way we measure time today with clocks is completely artificial. Clock time exists only because of agreements people made.

The agreements are called Standard Time and it's pretty new. It was invented in 1883 and didn't become law in the United States until 1913.

Before then, the idea of noon was strictly a local thing. Whenever the sun got as high as it was going to get - that was high noon. And a sundial kept track of that perfectly well.

Beakman
Beakman Place

Standard Time Versus Natural Time

WHAT YOU NEED: Stick - sunny day - 10 or 12 rocks - clock

WHAT TO DO: As soon as the sun comes up, stick your stick into the ground outside. Find the end of the stick's shadow and put a rock there.

Come back every hour and put a rock at the end of the shadow. Do this until the sun sets.

MORE STUFF: Keep track of which rock is what time. *You Can* use your sundial instead of a clock.

Come back in about 2 weeks and see if *clock noon* is still at the rock it was 2 weeks ago.

SO WHAT: Your sundial works because the Earth rotates. That makes the Sun seem to travel across the sky. As the Sun seems to move, shadows move too. If you keep track of any shadow's movement, *You Can* keep track of time. And that's all a sundial does, track a moving shadow.

Standard Time does not vary with the time of year, or the seasons. But sundial time does change from day to day. That's why *clock noon* doesn't match *sundial noon* after a couple of weeks.

P.S. from Jax: Daniel also asked, *Is it magic?* If you're talking about the playing-tricks kind of magic, no, it's not magic. But if you're talking about something being really wonderful even after you understand it, yes - then it's magical.

Dear Beakman,

What is chocolate? How do you make it?

Emily Najar
San Antonio, Texas

Dear Emily,

Chocolate was first discovered and used by the ancient Mayans in Mexico. It was so valuable, they used it for money.

Chocolate is made by crushing the seeds of the cacao tree into a thick goo. The goo flavors all chocolate products - from chocolate kisses to ice cream.

The word chocolate is from the Mayan language, and it means sour water. That's because chocolate without added sugar is surprisingly bitter.

Beakman

Beakman Place

Make Some Mayan Chocolate

Grown-ups love chocolate as much as you do. Some of them will even admit it. *You Can* make a kind of chocolate that is a lot like a kind of chocolate still popular in Mexico today.

WHAT YOU NEED: Dry, unsweetened cocoa - sugar - shortening - microwave oven - aluminum foil

WHAT TO DO: Visit the grocery store to get the cocoa powder. Taste a bit of it, and you'll see why the Mayans named it after something that tastes sour.

Put 3 level tablespoons of the powder in a bowl. Add 2 tablespoons of sugar and 1½ tablespoons of shortening. ⚠ Put the bowl in the microwave and zap it on high for 2 minutes. Stop the oven every 30 seconds and stir it up really well with a fork. After you take it out, keep stirring.

Spoon out the paste onto a piece of foil that you have put on a plate. If you like, smoosh it into the shape of a heart.

Stick it in the fridge for 30 minutes. Peel off the foil and eat it. Or better still, give it to someone as a gift.

WHAT IS GOING ON:
Your chocolate is not milk chocolate. Milk chocolate is a lot finer and isn't gritty. That's because huge machines grind it up into a fine paste with dried milk.

The ancient Mayans lived in the Yucatan. The Maya people still live there today.

Chocolate Words

CACAO (ka-KAU-o) - The tree that grows cacao beans. Cacao beans (or seeds) grow in a big pod like a long cantaloupe.

CHOCOLATE LIQUOR - After the seeds are scooped out of their pod, they are set in the sun. Then they are ground up. The thick, gooey liquid they make is chocolate liquor. It's 54% fat.

COCOA (KO-ko) - Chocolate liquor is put in a huge press and the fat is squeezed out. The powder that's left is cocoa.

COCOA BUTTER - The fat in the cacao seeds/beans. It is thick, which is why it's called a butter.

MILK CHOCOLATE - Cocoa, cocoa butter, milk solids and sugar.

Chocolate is hard to make because the fat and the powder don't mix very well. Milton Hershey found out that if you add another ingredient - lecithin - the chocolate gets smooth. Hershey invented the chocolate kiss, which his mother used to wrap with foil. She was a very busy woman.

Dear Beakman,

Can you make square bubbles?

Jennifer West
Winnipeg,
Manitoba

Dear Jennifer,

Yes, *You Can* make a square bubble. But you have to force it.

Bubbles can teach you a lot about chemistry and geometry. Also, blowing weirdly shaped and extra-large bubbles is a lot of fun.

The bubble formula I have for you might upset 2 groups of people - the folks who sell it in those teeny tiny bottles, and your family, because of the mess.

Take the mess and the fun outside into the sun.

Beakman

Beakman Place

Beakman's Bubbles

Better and Lots Cheaper

WHAT YOU NEED: Liquid dishwashing soap - glycerine (from drugstore) - gallon jug - dishpan or other large flat pan, like a big cake pan

WHAT TO DO: Add $2/3$ cup of the soap to a gallon of water. Add the soap last so you don't get a jug full of suds. Add 1 tablespoon of glycerine, which will help your bubbles last longer. Ask the people at the drugstore for it. You may want to experiment by trying things like Jell-O, Certo or even sugar instead. I use glycerine.

IMPORTANT: The soap you use has to be clear or transparent. Do not use any lotion-type soaps. Also, the more expensive brands work better for bubbles. I use Dawn or Ajax, but *You Can* try others. Soap for a dishwashing machine won't work.

MORE STUFF TO DO: Stir it well and let the formula sit for a while. Pour several inches of it into your pan. When using the bubble tools you're going to make, make sure your hands are really wet with the formula. Ditto for the bubble tools. Bubbles break when something dry touches them - even a piece of dust. The way you think and behave is important, too. Be gentle and slow while learning to work with your tools. Then it's O.K. to get crazy and radical. If it's windy outside, come inside and work at the sink.

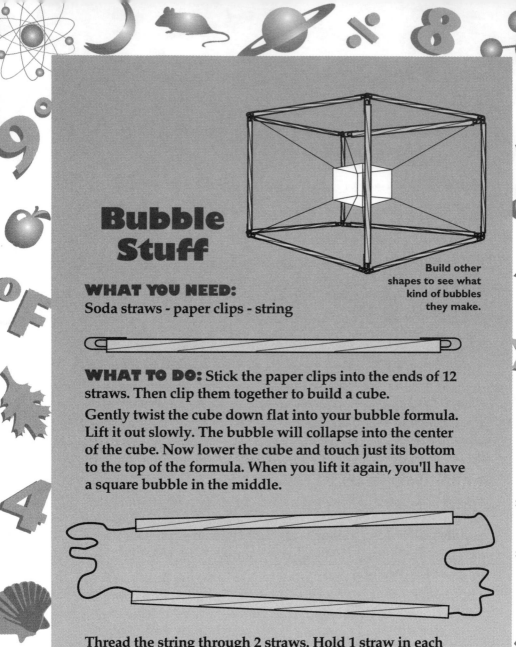

Bubble Stuff

Build other shapes to see what kind of bubbles they make.

WHAT YOU NEED:
Soda straws - paper clips - string

WHAT TO DO: Stick the paper clips into the ends of 12 straws. Then clip them together to build a cube.

Gently twist the cube down flat into your bubble formula. Lift it out slowly. The bubble will collapse into the center of the cube. Now lower the cube and touch just its bottom to the top of the formula. When you lift it again, you'll have a square bubble in the middle.

Thread the string through 2 straws. Hold 1 straw in each hand and dip the whole thing in your formula. Lift it out slowly. If you have a friend to help, *You Can* make this loop 5 or 6 feet long. Hold it out tight. Lift it in the wind.

P.S. from Jax: When you're done making bubbles, carefully pour your bubble formula back into the jug. *You Can* use it over and over again.

Dear Beakman,

How does milk turn into cheese?

Danielle Beck
San Francisco,
California

Dear Danielle,

The stuff that Little Miss Muffet was eating when the spider sat down beside her is the stuff that *You Can* make cheese out of: curds and whey.

Milk is not really just a liquid. Milk is made out of solid particles floating in liquid. Cheese is pretty much the solid particles from milk *without* the liquid.

You Can make a delicious cheese at home, and you don't have to know any spiders to do it.

Beakman
Beakman Place

Curdle Some Milk

WHAT YOU NEED: ½ cup homogenized milk - 2 tablespoons vinegar

WHAT TO DO: Put the first tablespoon of vinegar into the milk and stir it up. Use the spoon to ladle through the milk, lifting and pouring. Add the rest of the vinegar and keep ladling. Look carefully at the milk as it flows off the spoon. Vinegar is a kind of acid - acetic acid. What does it do to milk?

It takes about 11 pounds of milk to get enough curds to make 1 pound of cheese.

WHAT IS GOING ON: That was pretty awful, wasn't it? The milk got all lumpy and cruddy. Most important, it got thick, which is the first part of making cheese.

Added bacteria that eat the sugars in milk make another kind of acid as their waste - lactic acid - and it thickens milk.

Next, cheese-makers add rennet, which is a chemical discovered in the fourth stomach of cows. It separates milk into whey (WAY), the liquid; and curds, the solids.

Make Some Cheese

WHAT YOU NEED: Carton of non-fat cottage cheese (*NOT* low-fat) - salt - a favorite herb, like thyme - old white T-shirt - plenty of patience - permission and help from your family

WHAT TO DO: Mix 1 teaspoon of salt into the cottage cheese. Add ½ teaspoon of your herb. Mix this up really well.

Cut up the old T-shirt so that you have one flat piece of cloth - like the front or back of the shirt. Rinse the shirt in clear plain water and wring it out. Do this a couple of times.

Lay the cloth out and plop the cottage cheese onto it. Lift up the cloth and twist it tightly into a ball.

SALT of the

NON-FAT Cottage Cheese

THYME

Read more about cheese in the encyclopedia at your library.

Hang it in a cool place where a rank smell won't bother you - like a garage, or basement, or maybe a brother or sister's room. It's going to ooze and drip and smell for more than a week.

In 10 days, peel off the cloth and enjoy with crackers. You just made *farmer's cheese*.

P.S. from Jax: Non-fat cottage cheese is pretty much curds with most of the whey already drained. You just did the last part in cheese-making. You dried and aged the curds.

Dear Jax,

My dad just had a bypass operation. What is going on?

Jason Wilcox
Alameda,
California

Dear Jason,

Your heart works really, really hard. In 24 hours it does enough work to lift 130 tons. A fist-sized ball of muscles is doing that work - pumping blood used by the body for its work.

Heart muscles need blood, too. Especially since they work so hard. But the blood that's pumping *inside* the heart does not feed the heart's muscles.

Blood that gives oxygen to the heart's muscles flows through arteries and veins. If one of those gets clogged, the heart can't work, and the muscles get damaged. It's pretty scary stuff. Here's how a bypass helped your dad get better.

Jax Place

The Main Squeeze

Your heart is a ball of muscles that pumps blood by squeezing.

The muscles of the heart need blood to do their work, too.

It flows there through veins and arteries that must stay free of clogs.

If the heart muscles don't get the blood they need, they get damaged. We call that a heart attack.

Aorta
(a-OR-ta)

Bypass

Clog

Arteries

Veins

Mirror Message:
A double bypass means that the doctors sewed bypasses in 2 places. A triple bypass means they did it in 3.

Clogged Plumbing

Check out the drawing of the heart. All those veins and arteries on the outside of the heart carry the blood that the heart muscles need.

But they can get clogged with this junk called plaque (PLAK) which contains cholesterol (co-LES-tur-ol). Cholesterol is stuff that's in things from animals, like meat, eggs, milk or cheese.

Over years and years, this stuff can build up and form a plug in the pipes.

A bypass is when a surgeon sews in a piece of vein that *passes by* the clog. It brings in blood from the aorta.

Clog

Bypass

Not everyone gets clogged. (People who are addicted to tobacco do get more clogs.)

P.S. from Beakman: *You Can* work to keep yourself and your family healthy by exercising, eating less meat and by getting tobacco out of your home.

Dear Jax,

If you rub the powder off a butterfly's wings, will it really die?

Joe & Shelley Kendall
Valparaiso, Indiana

Dear Joe & Shelley,

That's practically a childhood legend. Everyone has heard that you'd kill a butterfly (or a moth) if you rubbed the *powder* from its wings. But hardly anyone knows why it's actually true.

That *powder* is really tiny little shingles all over the wings - like scales. Without them, the moth or butterfly cannot control its flying. It dies because we've accidentally taken away its ability to find food and shelter.

This is a terrific thing to do a report on at school. *You Can* even make a model of a moth or butterfly wing out of just paper and tape.

Jax Place
Jax Place

More Than They Seem

WHAT YOU NEED:
Paper - scissors - tape - crayons

WHAT TO DO: Cut lots of circles. Make them the size of a big coin, like a half-dollar. Then cut them in half. Color them any color you like.

MORE STUFF TO DO: Tape a row of the half-circles across the bottom of another piece of paper. Start a new row above the first, moved over just a bit, like in this drawing. Keep going until the paper is filled. If you like, use the colors to make a pattern.

SO WHAT: Take your project to school and see if anyone can figure out what it's supposed to be. Tell them it's a butterfly wing. When they say you must be really dumb, pull out an encyclopedia and show them a picture to prove it. Blow air over the wing. What happens?

Butterflies — Up Close and Personal

Some schools have microscopes. Some do not. If your school has one, take a moth or a butterfly to class to inspect under the lens. You'll think you're looking at a rooftop covered with shingles. The scales are only on the wing tops.

The scales help the moth or butterfly control the way air flows over its wings. Airplanes use flaps called ailerons (AY-leh-ronz) to do the same thing. If moths or butterflies can't fly right, they can't live - so they die.

P.S. from Beakman: All butterflies and moths have a fancy last name - Lepidoptera (lep-eh-DOP-tur-a). It's from 2 Greek words. It means scaly wings!

Dear Beakman,

When you dream, are you able to read in your dream?

**Timothy Huber
Dodgeville,
Wisconsin**

Dear Timothy,

At certain times of year, like Halloween, I get a lot of questions about weird stuff like ghosts and dreams. The only answer I can give you is that *You Can* read while you're dreaming if you're dreaming that you're reading.

See, dreams and dreaming are not things that happen to us. Dreams are something we make up for ourselves. No one can tell you what you can or cannot dream. It's up to you. Really.

Beakman
Beakman Place

Playing With Words

WHAT YOU NEED: Pencil - paper - active imagination - help from your family

WHAT TO DO: Go into any room of your home. Divide the paper into 2 columns. Ask someone to pick out any object in the room. Write down its name in the first column.

In the second column, write down all the things it reminds you of. This is where you need your imagination and help. *You Can* come up with at least 10 things any 1 thing reminds you of. Do all this for 5 items. It'll be a fun thing to do together.

SO WHAT: You just acted out the difference between your conscious (KAHN-shus) and unconscious (un-KAHN-shus) minds. Our conscious mind keeps track of very literal stuff, like a thing's name. Your unconscious is a bit more playful and isn't limited by things like time and space. It can list very wild and unexpected things.

When you go to sleep, your conscious mind is shut down for the night. That leaves the unconscious mind free to party. That's what your dreams are - your unconscious mind going over your list in a free-form, playful kind of way.

dish | dinner
sink
dishpan-hands
wheel
rolling
frisbee
kitty
tuna

59

Direct Your Dreams

WHAT YOU NEED: Just your sweet self

WHAT TO DO: Pick a color that you'd like to see in a dream. As you fall asleep, think of all the things that color reminds you of. Keep adding to the list of things your color reminds you of until you fall asleep.

SO WHAT: If you keep doing this, night after night, you will eventually see your color in your dream. You'll also know that it's there because you wanted it to be there. And it will feel great!

P.S. from Jax: Directing your own dreams takes time. Be patient with yourself. And keep working at it.

Dear Jax,

How come a car horn sounds low when it's far away and high-pitched when it's closer?

**Laura Arnold
Akron, Ohio**

Dear Laura,

Close your eyes and imagine it's night and a train whistle travels by. Then think about it a moment. It's not the distance that matters; it's the movement.

Sound waves are like little pushes of air. When the thing making the sound is moving toward you, the pushes get pushed together even tigher and the pitch goes up.

When it moves away from you, the opposite thing happens and the pitch goes down. It's called the Doppler effect.

Jax Place
Jax Place

Capturing Doppler on Tape

WHAT YOU NEED: Tape recorder with microphone - something that makes noise like a car horn or an electric razor - permission and help from your family

WHAT TO DO: Start the noise and tape-record some of it. Turn off the noise and listen to the tape. It should sound the same. Do it again, only this time hold the microphone at the end of your outstretched arm and make wide sweeping arcs. Hold it as far away as *You Can* and swing your arm right up close to the sound. Do it a couple of times. Pretend your microphone is a Jedi's Lightsaber. Listen to that tape.

WHAT IS GOING ON: This technique was first used by sound designer Ben Burtt to add a sense of motion to the sound effect for the Lightsaber in the *Star Wars* movies. By measuring the change in pitch, you would be able to tell how fast the microphone moved.

That's how police radar works to measure the speed of cars. Instead of sound waves, radio waves (radar) are bounced off moving cars. The change in their pitch can tell the police how fast the car was moving.

P.S. from Jax: The Doppler effect can also affect light. That's how astronomers can tell how fast stars are moving away from Earth - by measuring the shift in the color of starlight.

Dear Jax,

How does the Internet work?

James Coates
Windsor, Ontario

Dear James,

It's important to remember that the Internet is only computers talking to each other on telephone lines - the same phone lines you use to talk on. In fact, just about any time you use the phone, you're sharing the phone line with computer data.

More than 10 million computers share phone lines by converting the data into lots of little chunks called *data packets*. Stuff like your e-mail or the pictures on the Web move from computer to computer in thousands of little chunks - all like little cars sharing the same roads.

Jax Place
Jax Place

15 Milliseconds of Fame

Each packet is a self-contained unit with enough information to move through the phone lines all by itself. Once done traveling, packets join up with their brother-and-sister packets and become e-mail, World Wide Web pictures or other files.

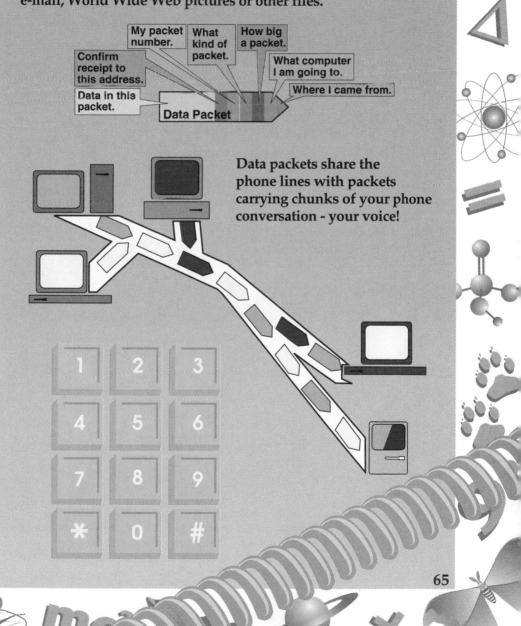

My packet number.

What kind of packet.

How big a packet.

Confirm receipt to this address.

What computer I am going to.

Data in this packet.

Where I came from.

Data Packet

Data packets share the phone lines with packets carrying chunks of your phone conversation - your voice!

Alphabet Soup

URL	**http://www.beakman.com/interact/demo.html**
URL	**U**niform **R**esource **L**ocator - World Wide Web address
http:	**H**yper **T**ext **T**ransmission **P**rotocol - The way www data is sent over phone lines
www	**W**orld **W**ide **W**eb - Millions of Hypertext files linked together
.html	**H**yper **T**ext **M**ark-up **L**anguage - The code that's used to build a www page. A kind of file to transfer.
.com	A kind of domain. .com means it's commercial - a business.
.org	This domain is for nonprofit organizations.
.edu	Colleges or universities
.ca	Canadian domains (.uk-England, .de-Germany, .nl-Netherlands, etc.)
/	This separates directory names. The file *demo.html* is inside a directory called *interact*.

jok@nbn.com	
jok	The user's log-on
@	The "at" symbol
nbn	Domain where user is *at*
.com	Kind of domain

Internet addresses must be 1 word only, so periods are used as place-holders. They're called *dots*.

P.S. from Beakman: Movable type made it possible for most everyone to read books. That was 500 years ago. The Internet allows most everyone to publish anything they want. That's another big change, and we don't yet know how the world will change because of it.

Dear Jax,

Why is it when you are wet, you seem to be colder than when you are dry?

**Luke Anderson
Davenport,
Washington**

Dear Luke,

That sounds like a shivering-beside-the-swimming-pool, where's-the-towel, teeth-chattering question. It sends a chill up my spine just to think about it. (You might get one in a couple of seconds.)

The water on your skin needs heat energy to dry. That energy is going to come from you, from your body heat.

You feel colder because heat moves from you to the water on your skin, which makes it possible for the water to turn into a gas and float away. When it does float away, it takes that heat along for the ride.

Jax Place
Jax Place

Turning a Liquid into Gas

WHAT YOU NEED: A grown-up - rubbing alcohol - tissue

WHAT TO DO: ⚠Rubbing alcohol can be very dangerous stuff, so get a grown-up to help. Grown-ups like to think they are teaching you something. They enjoy that and will lend a hand. Ask for help working with the alcohol.

Rub an alcohol-soaked tissue onto the back of your hand.

Gently blow. Watch the wet spots as you blow, and feel the temperature of your hand.

SO WHAT: Your hand felt like ice, and *evaporation* is the reason why. Evaporation is when a liquid turns into a gas. That's what happens when something dries. Cold alcohol will not evaporate (ee-VAP-or-ate). The heat it needed came from your hand. As the alcohol drifted away, it took the heat from your hand with it. Water does the same thing, only slower. Both make you cold.

Hospitals used to use alcohol to cool down people with fevers. It was rubbed on patients' skin, which is why it's called *rubbing* alcohol.

P.S. from Beakman: The reason you see those wavy lines on the bottom of the pool is that water bends light. The sunlight is bent and unbent as waves and ripples float by on the top of the water. An artist named David Hockney likes to make pictures of them.

Turning a Gas into Liquid

WHAT YOU NEED: Warm tea -
2 glasses - ice

WHAT TO DO: Do this outside on a muggy day. Pour warm tea into 1 of the glasses until it's ⅓ full. Feel the outside of the glass. Next, fill the glass with enough ice to make iced tea. When it's really cold, look at the outside of the glass.

Use the second glass to make a nice glass of iced tea for a friend.

SO WHAT: This is the opposite of Experiment #1. The warm glass was dry. When you added ice, the cold glass absorbed heat from the air. This chilled the air next to the glass, and cold air cannot hold very much water vapor, a gas. The water vapor had to turn back into a liquid, which formed all those wet drips on the outside of the glass.

Dear Raymond,

Feet smell and feet sometimes smell bad. Feet smell because animals, including humans, produce chemicals that identify us as individuals. They are called pheromones (FAIR-eh-moans). Feet smell bad when very tiny plants or animals grow on our skin. It sounds gross, but it's true. They are called microbes (MY-kroabs), which means small life. They are everywhere and *You Can* grow some at home.

Beakman

Beakman Place

We All Have Our Own Unique Smell

EXPERIMENT #1

WHAT YOU NEED: A friend - a blindfold - a quiet time - permission from your family

WHAT TO DO: Sit down in the living room and put on the blindfold. Don't peek. Tell your friend to go around the house and take a T-shirt out of everyone's clothes dresser - one each for every member of your family. You should stay quiet and get relaxed. Your friend will let you smell each shirt. Without touching the shirts, *You Can* still tell whose shirt it is just by the smell. Now try it at your friend's house.

The nose knows!

WHAT IS GOING ON: We all have our own unique smell - something that is ours alone and different from anyone else. We get used to these smells and don't think about it much. That's why you should relax and be quiet when you do this. Our smells even change the fragrance of perfume or cologne. That's why it's a little different on every person. It's also the reason different houses smell different. The smell comes from the pheromones we make.

The Unseen World

There are plants and animals so small we need a microscope to see them. There are billions and billions of them, and they live everywhere - even on us. They even live inside us.

The microbes that make feet smell bad have very long names. One is called *Brevibacteria-linen*. Another is *Corybacteria JK*. They are both kind of like family names. Many microbes are members of those families, and when they grow they're smelly.

We can wash some of them off. But microbes duplicate on and on, so we can't ever get rid of them. When something has been cleaned of all microbes, we say that it's sterile. But microbes always get back in eventually. Microbes are just about everywhere - at least on this planet. We are protected from most of the bad ones by our bodies' immune systems.

71

Growing Microbes

WHAT YOU NEED: Clean mayonnaise jar - unflavored gelatin - cotton swab - water - patience

WHAT TO DO: Boil 1/2 cup water, sprinkle in 4 envelopes unflavored gelatin. Dissolve it. Pour into the mayonnaise jar and set the jar on its side. Let the extra pour out. Put on sneakers without socks and go play outside. Three hours later, the gelatin will be hard and your feet will be smelly. This is a great experiment to do at school. Collect your microbes after recess or gym. Take the swab and rub it well in between all your toes. Now carefully brush the gelatin with the cotton tip in long strokes. Close the jar and put it in a warm, dark spot. Leave it there 4 whole days. Go wash your feet.

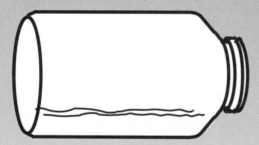

WHAT IS GOING ON: Inside your shoes it's dark, warm and damp - perfect for microbes! And they grow and grow. Your jar is pretty much the same. The gelatin is what the microbes are eating. It is called a growth medium. After 4 days, you'll be able to see grooves in the gelatin. The microbes are eating it. When you open it, you'll smell something much worse than smelly feet. It smells horrible. Really. Don't keep the jar any longer and don't touch it inside. Fill it with hot water, let it soak and then recycle the jar. Wash your hands!

Microbes grow even when we don't want them to. That's why the forgotten thing in the back of the refrigerator looks all gross, smelly and hairy. It is not a Science Fair project. It's microbes.

Dear Beakman,

What are feathers made from?

Marie Schumacher
Kenosha,
Wisconsin

Dear Marie,

Well, feathers have lots to do with both protein and zippers. Feathers are made of the same protein our hair is made from, keratin (CARE-eh-tin). Feathers are pretty much *hair with zippers*.

Beakman
Beakman Place

73

Kinds of Feathers - A Closer Look

WHAT YOU NEED: Feather - feather pillow

WHAT TO DO: *You Can* find a feather on sidewalks or in yards. They're all over the place because birds lose them. Compare one to the tiny fluffy feathers that leak out of a pillow. If you live near a farm, these fluffy feathers can be found near chicken coops or duck ponds. *You Can* even find them leaking out of down sleeping bags or down jackets. Both the feather and the fluff are feathers. But what's the difference? Examine both closely. Compare what's different and the same.

A
Hooked barbule

B
Barbule

Barb

MORE STUFF: Take the larger feather and pull apart the side. Now use your fingers to zip it back together again. Start at the quill and *zipper* out to the edge of the feather.

SO WHAT: Feathers are a lot like hair and fish scales. All are made of keratin. But only feathers have branches that we call *barbs*. Each barb looks like a tiny *feather* itself. These barbs have smaller branches called *barbules* (BAR-byools).

Birds have two different kinds of feathers. The big ones are called *contour feathers*, and the fluffy ones are called *down*. The big difference between them is their barbules. Diagrams A & B are not feathers; they are the branches of feathers. Diagram A is a contour feather barb. Diagram B is down. Down doesn't hook onto itself. It's soft and fluffy. Contour feathers are different. They have hooks on their barbules. The hooks make feathers like hair with zippers. Those hooks are why *You Can* repair a split feather with your fingers.

P.S. from Jax: When you see a bird combing itself with its beak, what it's really doing is zipping its feathers back together again.

Dear Jax,

What are the laws of the Universe?

**Lee Chatham
Woodbury, Tennessee**

Dear Lee,

That's kind of a mind-expanding question! The best questions are the ones that make you think a bit. And Beakman and I thought *a lot* about this one.

Genius Nobel Prize–winning physicists like Leon Lederman are out looking for *the one law* of the Universe.

But when we answer questions, we keep seeing the same powerful laws pop up over and over. Today's comic might seem all cosmic, but the Universe is a pretty cosmic (and comic) place to be.

Jax Place

THE UNIVERSE LIKES BALANCE 1

The Universe working toward balance is why airplanes fly, why balloons lose their air, how fish can get oxygen from water, how batteries work, why the wind blows and lots more. Balance is needed for there to be matter. If an atom wasn't balanced, it couldn't exist. The forces of nature will push tirelessly and forever to make things balanced. Yow!

NOTHING EVER DISAPPEARS 2

There is only so much stuff in the universe. None of it disappears, ever. When things seem to disappear, they've really only changed their form. Like fire. Where did the wood go? It mixed with oxygen and transformed into other gases, the particles in the smoke and even into light and heat. An important part of this law is that energy is just another way for matter to be, and vice versa. Radical!

3 — THERE IS NO DARKNESS ONLY LIGHT

You cannot make something that is not a thing. Negative things like darkness or cold are not really things at all. They're the *absence* of things.

There is only more or less light. There is only more or less heat. To make dark you must block the light. To make cold you must remove the heat.

Energy will move into cold or dark spaces until all of the space shares equal light, equal heat. See Law #1.

4 — THERE ARE DIFFERENT TRUTHS

Energy can be a wave, like a radio wave or a light wave. A whole set of laws of nature flow from energy being a wave. But energy can also seem to be a *quantum* —a little chunk, or particle of energy. Photons are particles, chunks of light. And whole new laws flow from the view that energy is in chunks. We call this view *quantum mechanics*. Both views are *way different*. Both are completely true. They are different truths.

P.S. from Beakman: Behind #1 is the symbol for balance. Behind #2 is the symbol for infinity. Because of Law #4, we know that you might have different laws of the Universe. And they're all true, too!

Dear Beakman,

How do comics get their colors?

Mark Murray
Arnold, Maryland

Dear Mark,

All the colors in the Sunday funnies are made from only four different colored inks. Each ink is printed one at a time on top of each other, and the colors mix.

Grab the Sunday funnies. You'll need them for the experiment *You Can* do to learn about comics in color.

Beakman
Beakman Place

Fooling the Brain

WHAT YOU NEED: Color comics - clear tape - water   *Optional: Magnifying glass*

WHAT TO DO: Find the color green in the Sunday funnies. Cover it with tape. Press it down tight. Put one drop of water on top. Now look closely at the green through the water. Try it with other colors.

Grass green is 35% cyan (si-ANN) and 50% yellow. Magnified, it looks something like this.

WHAT IS GOING ON: The drop of water acted like a little magnifying glass, and the dots seem bigger. Newspapers aren't supposed to fool us. But printing does. Our brains get fooled. We can't see the dots as separate things, so cyan (light blue) and yellow dots get mixed together, and we see green. Now try the tape and water drops with *FoxTrot* or *Blondie* or *Cathy* or other color comics.

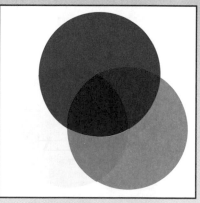

The inks are transparent. The colors mix and we get new colors.

80

It's All Done with Little Dots

Color printing uses little dots of just four colors to make all the colors you see. Look very closely at this chart. The dots are so big at the left that they touch. When they get smaller, the color gets weaker.

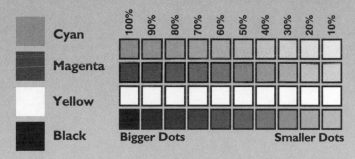

	100%	90%	80%	70%	60%	50%	40%	30%	20%	10%
Cyan										
Magenta										
Yellow										
Black										

Bigger Dots — Smaller Dots

Putting It Together

At the printing plant, printers put each color on separately. The rainbow pattern below is Beakman's tie. It's made by sending a piece of paper through a press that first puts on cyan, then magenta, then yellow and lastly, black. By themselves the separate inks don't look like much. Together, they look great. CMYK is printer talk for color. The K stands for black.*

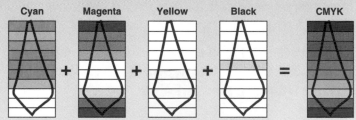

Cyan + Magenta + Yellow + Black = CMYK

*I know the word Black doesn't start with the letter K. But in a printing plant, K still means the color Black. The reason it's not B, is that B might be confused with the color Blue. The letter K doesn't turn up in the name of any other color. That's why K stands for black.

Dear Beakman,

Why will an egg float in salt water and won't float in regular water?

Jamie Hoyt
Tacoma,
Washington

Dear Jamie,

The egg-in-salt water trick is sometimes called *magic*. But if you explain a magic trick, it isn't magic anymore. That can make things confusing.

The egg trick is not magic. The answer to your question has to do with *density* (DENS-it-tee).

A floating thing is not as dense as the thing it's floating in. A thing sinks when it's more dense than the thing it sinks in.

Beakman

Beakman Place

Making Water More Dense

WHAT YOU NEED: Salt - water - glass - marking pen

WHAT TO DO: Fill the glass half-full of water. Mark the water line with the pen. Stir in as much salt as *You Can* dissolve. It will be a lot - 12 to 15 teaspoons.

Does the water line stay the same? Does it go up by as much salt as you added?

It's Not Magic; It's Real

WHAT YOU NEED: Salt water from Experiment #1 - 2 eggs - 2 glasses - water

WHAT TO DO: Put equal amounts of fresh water and salt water into the 2 glasses. Fill them to be half-full.

Now gently place an egg into each of the glasses. The egg in the salt water should float. The egg in the fresh water should sink. It's not magic. The salt water is more dense than the egg, so the egg floats.

What Is Going On

Density matters. A glass of fresh water weighs a certain amount. When you added 12 to 15 teaspoons of salt, the amount of water did *not* change - the size of the water did *not* change.

What *did change* was the salt made the water heavier. When you make something heavier and keep it the same size, you *increase its density*.

Fresh water   **Salt water**

Now your water is salt water and it's *more dense* than fresh water. Salt water is more dense than an egg, so it can hold up an egg. The egg will float.

Fresh water is not as dense as an egg, so the water cannot hold it up. The egg sinks in fresh water.

P.S. from Jax: It's not just eggs! Ships and everything else that floats will float easier in salt water - even people! Salt water is more dense than fresh water and holds swimmers up better.

Dear Jax,

Why do hurricane winds go so fast?

**Latonya Munson
Dallas, Texas**

Dear Latonya,

A hurricane is a huge storm system that is called a typhoon (ti-FOON) in other parts of the world.

Hurricane winds are so strong because of a special shape that concentrates motion.

It's a vortex (VOR-teks). You see a vortex when you flush a toilet or watch the water twirl down a sink drain. A vortex is like a swirling funnel. It takes a little bit of motion spread out over a big area and turns it into lots of motion packed into a little, tiny area.

Jax Place
Jax Place

85

Hurricane or Himicane?

WHAT YOU NEED: Large clear plastic soda bottle - potato - soda straw or tube from a ballpoint pen - help from a grown-up - water - place to make a mess

WHAT TO DO: Ask your grown-up helper to slice the potato into 1-inch-thick slices. Fill the bottle ¾ full with water. Put a slice of potato on top of the bottle. Twist it back and forth gently until it's seated like a cork. Use the straw or pen-tube to drill a hole through the potato slice. Twist the straw back and forth until it drills through.

The center of the vortex is empty and calm.

Make the hole in your potato this big.

MORE STUFF: You'll have to drill several times to get a hole the same size as the sample hole. Hold the potato on the bottle and turn it upside down. Swirl the whole thing in a light circular motion. The vortex will form as the water drains out.

SO WHAT: The movement in the water has to go somewhere. It *cannot* disappear. It ends up swirling the water at the bottom of the vortex very fast. You could power it in a different way if you could lift the center of the vortex up and let the water rush into where it was. That's how a hurricane works - the same shape vortex, but powered by the center of the storm lifting up.

All the motion and all the force of the winds at the top of the storm are concentrated by the hurricane's vortex. In your soda bottle, the falling water powers the vortex. In a hurricane, the center of the vortex is lifting up, causing the winds to rush in.

The motion from hundreds of square miles of the storm's top is focused around the center of the vortex, where winds can blow over 100 mph.

Looking down into the vortex from a satellite. This hurricane was more than 390 miles across. The winds rush in toward the center of the vortex and their power is concentrated.

P.S. from Beakman: *You Can* push a straw through a potato if you're real quick about it. Try it by counting one, two, three, go!

Dear Jax,
Why does eating asparagus make your urine smell funny?

Tom Scott
San Rafael,
California

Dear Tom,

When we put food into our bodies, we're putting raw materials into a chemical factory.

Our digestive system takes apart the chemicals that are in food and uses the pieces to put together new chemicals our bodies need. The stuff it doesn't need, or is done using, is thrown out as waste.

Asparagus gives our bodies an amino acid that we have to take apart before we can use it. What's left is what's causing the smell.

Jax Place
Jax Place

Soluble Test

WHAT YOU NEED: 2 clear glasses - 2 spoons - box of salt - really hot water - really cold water

WHAT TO DO: Put the hot and cold water in separate glasses. Use the spoons to measure out spoonfuls of salt. Stir them into the glasses of water until you can't add any more salt. Count how many spoonfuls *You Can* dissolve in hot water and how many you can dissolve in cold water. The number will be different. Cold water isn't as good at dissolving stuff as hot water.

SO WHAT: More salt was soluble in hot water than in cold water. When your body is digesting asparagus, it throws out a chemical called methyl mercaptan. It's dissolved in your warm urine. When the urine cools in the toilet bowl, some of it undissolves and *You Can* smell it.

ALL ABOUT ASPARAGUS

- Asparagus is a member of the lily plant family.
- Asparagus is a sprout. If you don't pick it, it'll end up turning into a big, fluffy, fernlike plant.
- Asparagus ferns are not really ferns. They're much like the plant you'd get if you didn't harvest asparagus.
- Asparagus is expensive because it has to be harvested by hand. It doesn't sprout at the same time or grow at the same rate.
- Asparagus contains an amino acid called methionine. When our bodies take that chemical apart, we get methyl mercaptan - the chemical with the strong fragrance.
- Not everyone can smell methyl mercaptan. Some people lack a gene in their DNA (their body's blueprints) that lets them notice the smell.

P.S. from Beakman: White asparagus is grown under heavy canvas in the dark. White bean sprouts and white endive are grown the same way - without sunshine.

Dear Charles,

Equinox is a very old word. It's based on the old language Latin, and it means *equal night*. On the equinox, daytime and nighttime are the same time long. Isn't that cosmic?

The equinox marks the change of seasons. When in the Northern Hemisphere it's the vernal equinox (spring), in the Southern Hemisphere it's the autumnal equinox (fall).

Beakman

Beakman Place

Globe Gazing: A Closer Look

Tropic of Cancer

Equator

Tropic of Capricorn

WHAT YOU NEED: Classroom globe - cooperative teacher

WHAT TO DO: If your class doesn't have a globe, the first thing to do is have a bake sale. Then use the money to buy a globe.

Next, use the drawing to the right as a guide to copy a year's travel around the Sun.

Push all the desks out to the edge of the room (this is where having a fun teacher is important). Choose someone to be the Sun and put the Sun in the center of the room where he or she can be all radiant.

Look at the 3 black lines across the Earth. The middle line is the *equator*. It's halfway between the North and South Poles. The top line is called the *Tropic of Cancer*. The bottom line is called the *Tropic of Capricorn*. Between the top and bottom lines is called being *in the Tropics*.

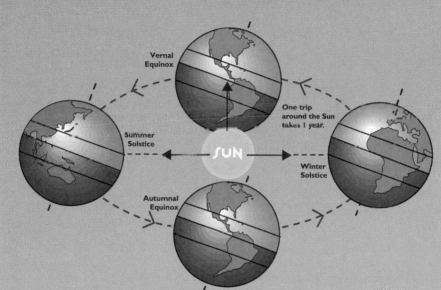

Mother Earth is like a gigantic clock. One of the ways she keeps time is the Sun's path moving up and down in the sky.

When the path is low, we have winter; when it's high, we have summer. When it's in the middle, we have autumn or spring, and those times are called the equinox!

The equinox is the moment when the Sun's daily high point is directly over the Earth's equator.

Hold the globe and walk in a circle around the Sun. Make sure that you hold the globe so that the axis is leaning in the same direction all the way around, *just like in the drawing*.

Your classmates should watch and help you figure out which season you're in as you circle the Sun.

P.S. from Jax: Vernal is another old word. It means green. The vernal equinox is the green equinox - springtime!

Dear Guys,

Diamonds are so hard because of the shape of a diamond's structure. Diamonds are pure carbon crystals. Each carbon atom is held tightly by four bonds to other carbon atoms nearby. It's a very strong shape.

This a great question for a Cub Scout den because *You Can* build a model of a diamond structure together. The stuff you use to build the diamond model is Cub Scout soul-food. So after you learn, *You Can* eat your experiment!

Beakman
Beakman Place

WHAT YOU NEED: Bag of marshmallows - round toothpicks - helpful den leader *(like yours, Mr. Rick) Optional: Gumdrops*

Build a dozen or so of these to start. Push the toothpicks *all the way* into the marshmallow. Use your imagination to connect the ends of the toothpicks.

The shape you'd get is called a tetrahedron (tet-rah-HE-dron). It's like a tripod and is a very strong shape.

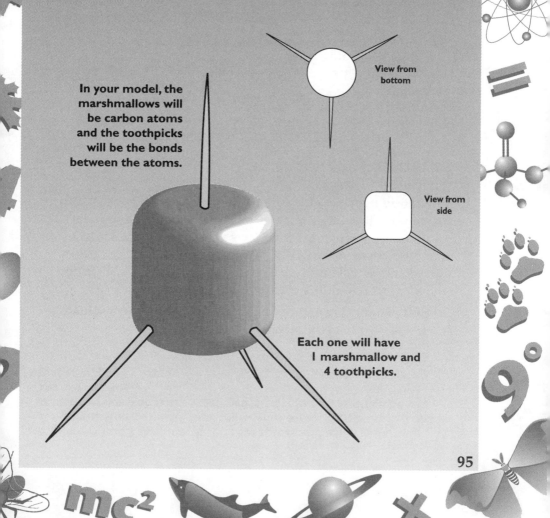

In your model, the marshmallows will be carbon atoms and the toothpicks will be the bonds between the atoms.

View from bottom

View from side

Each one will have 1 marshmallow and 4 toothpicks.

95

What a Bunch of Marshmallows!

WHAT TO DO: Look at the big drawing and build a lot of these. Then use the marshmallows you have left to stack them up. Every time toothpicks come together, anchor them with a marshmallow. Start with a triangle-shaped base of 15 tetrahedrons with 5 to each side of the triangle. Anchor the bottom legs together and start building upward. If you use gumdrops instead of marshmallows, you'll get a much stronger model.

SO WHAT:

Your model is a bit wobbly because marshmallows are soft and gooshy. But you can use it to see what a strong structure these shapes would make if the marshmallows were hard. That's why diamonds are so very hard - because of the shape the carbon atoms make attached to each other in this way. When carbon atoms are attached in a different shape, they're soft.

Graphite is another kind of carbon. It's in your pencil lead, and it's so soft it's slippery.

P.S. from Jax: Take out all the toothpicks and ask a grown-up for permission to roast your marshmallows. The black stuff on the outside of roasted marshmallows is carbon that used to be a part of the sugar!

Dear Beakman,

Why do people fart?

Bert Songprasit

Mays Landing, New Jersey

Dear Bert,

This is one of those rude word questions that I might get in trouble for talking about. Still, it's an excellent question - one lots of people wonder about. The polite word for it is flatulence (FLA-chu-lentz). There are usually polite words for unpolite subjects. It makes some of us feel better to have them around, even if we don't use them much. Flatulence is mostly air mixed with the gas methane. Other gases mixed in are the stuff that make farts smell. Methane doesn't smell. Really.

Beakman

Beakman Place

Sometimes It's Loud - Sometimes It Isn't

EXPERIMENT #1

WHAT YOU NEED: Just yourself

WHAT TO DO: Hold your lips tight together - as tight as *You Can*. Take a big breath. Now fill up your cheeks with the air. Keep pressing with your lungs while you try to keep your lips shut. What happened? Now try it again, only relax your lips.

WHAT IS GOING ON: There are ring-shaped muscles all along our digestive system. They open and close all the time without our knowing about it. They are called sphincters (SFINK-turs). It is a proper word, but it still makes grown-ups squirm. So don't use it around them. If you hold those ring muscles tight, it'll be loud when you pass gas. If your ring muscles are relaxed it will be quiet.

Stuff to Do to Understand

EXPERIMENT #2

WHAT TO DO: Brush your teeth.

WHY: The toothpaste is pushed along the tube and out to your brush. That's how food and gas move through our digestive system.

WHAT TO DO: Use the hose to wash your car.

WHY: The hose will spurt when you first turn it on. The water is pushing out air just like your body pushes out gas.

We're All Long Tubes

This is a simple drawing of our insides. You might say these are our guts. The first thing that makes gas is our stomach. We make acids there to start breaking down food. Pour some vinegar on a bit of baking soda. It will make gas a lot like our stomach does. That gas is a burp.

By the time food gets to our intestines, it is a paste. Microbes that live in our intestines start breaking down the paste that hasn't yet been absorbed by our body. When microbes do that, methane gas is made. The bad smell comes from foods that contain chemicals like sulfur - like eggs, onions and beans. The blue dashes in the drawing are pockets of gas forming in our guts. It has to go somewhere. It gets pushed out our rear end.

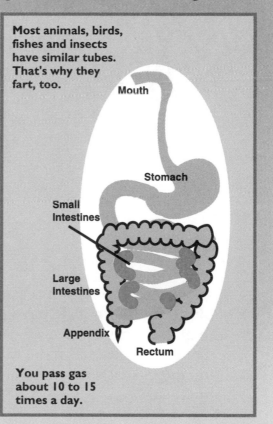

Most animals, birds, fishes and insects have similar tubes. That's why they fart, too.

Mouth

Stomach

Small Intestines

Large Intestines

Appendix

Rectum

You pass gas about 10 to 15 times a day.

The gas you cook or heat with was made the same way our body makes gas. The Earth has pockets of gas made by microbes that digested plants and animals millions of years ago. I guess when they call it natural gas, they're right.

Dear Beakman,

How do glasses help us to see better?

Laura Hargitt
West Jordan, Utah

Dear Laura,

There are a lot of things our eyes have to do perfectly for us to have perfect sight. If just one of those things is not quite right, we need glasses. But the glasses have to be made just for you and your unique eyes.

Eyeglasses work by bending light beams so that they meet right at the back of our eyeballs on the retina (RET-in-ah). The retina changes light into signals that go to the brain.

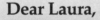

Beakman

Beakman Place

A Look Inside Your Looker

A Whole Lot Going On

Our eyeballs work a lot like little cameras. There is a lens that focuses the light. Light has to focus exactly at the retina for our sight to be clear.

The first thing that can go wrong is the length of the eyeball. It can be too short or too long. Or the cornea can have the wrong shape. The lenses in our eyeglasses help the lenses in our eyes. They make sure the light focuses right at the retina so we can see clearly.

When we look at faraway things, the lens is pulled flat by little muscles. When we look at close things, the muscles pull in and the lens gets fat and round. The idea is to keep everything in focus.

Retina

Muscle

Cornea

Lens

Muscle

EXPERIMENT #1

Different Glasses Fix Different Problems

WHAT YOU NEED: a few friends who wear glasses (perhaps your classmates at school)

WHAT TO DO: Hold a pair of glasses out at the end of your arm. Look at the view. Look at the lenses, too. Look at several different pairs. Be very careful not to hurt the glasses. People who wear glasses need them to see well. Respect that. If you wear glasses, keep yours on when it's your turn.

WHAT IS GOING ON:

Different kinds of seeing problems need different kinds of lenses that bend light differently. Here are some examples:

Glasses for farsighted people: These lenses will make the view look bigger or even upside down. When people are farsighted they can see far. They cannot see things clearly that are close up. One cause of it is eyeballs that are too short.

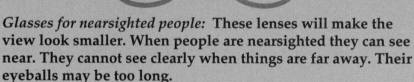

Glasses for nearsighted people: These lenses will make the view look smaller. When people are nearsighted they can see near. They cannot see clearly when things are far away. Their eyeballs may be too long.

Glasses for people with astigmatism: These will change the shape of the view, stretching it out and maybe twisting it. People with astigmatism (ah-STIG-ma-tis-m) have a cornea that is out of shape. The weird stretched-out lens fixes it.

P.S. from Jax: If you know people in their 40s, you may see one of them hold the newspaper at the end of their arms to read. Their lens muscles are weaker and can't focus closely anymore. Mention reading glasses to them.

Dear Jax,

Why does cinnamon taste hot and mint taste cool?

Eric Hanson
Dallas, Texas

Dear Eric,

Cinnamon and mint do not change the temperature in your mouth. You're getting all irritated or fooled.

The chemicals in cinnamon that seem to be hot are phenolic compounds. They're in the cinnamon tree to protect it.

The chemical in mint that seems cool is menthol. Menthol isn't cool; it just fools your mouth's nerves into giving your brain a false signal for cool.

Jax Place
Jax Place

It's Not Breakfast. It's Empirical Research!

WHAT YOU NEED: Toasted bread - cinnamon - sugar - active imagination

WHAT TO DO: Sprinkle lots and lots of cinnamon all over the toast. Don't be stingy. Don't add any sugar.

Close your eyes. Imagine you're a bug. You're flying through Southeast Asian jungles looking for something to eat. You see this delicious-looking tree ahead. You fly right up to the tree and chomp right into its bark. Quick! Take a big bite of your toast!

Add the sugar and
enjoy the rest of your toast.

SO WHAT: *Empirical* means to learn by doing. And you just learned empirically that cinnamon's taste can keep bugs away. It tasted pretty bad without the sugar we usually add. Plants seem to use phenolics to keep away microbes and bugs.

Strong concentrations of phenolic compounds can irritate the cells inside your mouth, which get flushed with blood as the body tries to carry away the irritant. When it's strong enough, it feels like a burn. That's why cinnamon can seem *hot*. It's how salsa works, too.

Cinnamon is tree bark from the *Cinnamomum zeylanicum* tree that grows in Sri Lanka. What we call cinnamon in the United States is really bark from the cassia, a related tree that grows in Myanmar (Burma). Thin strips of bark curl up when they dry. They are called *bark quills.*

Plants in the *Mentha labiatae* family make the chemical menthol. There are dozens of different kinds of mints. The plant grows just about anywhere and grows so well it takes over a garden like a weed.

P.S. from Beakman: The reason cassia is sold instead of real cinnamon is that people think it tastes more like cinnamon than real cinnamon. Go figure!

Dear Justin,

Bridges don't fall because of their structure. Different shapes behave differently. They do different things when weight is placed on them.

Two very strong shapes are used a lot in bridges: triangles and arches.

Beakman

Beakman Place

Triangles vs. Squares

WHAT YOU NEED: Drinking straws - paper clips - scissors

WHAT TO DO: Cut 7 straws to about $\frac{3}{4}$ their original length. Put a paper clip into each end of the straws. Then start hooking them together. Make shapes like in the diagrams.

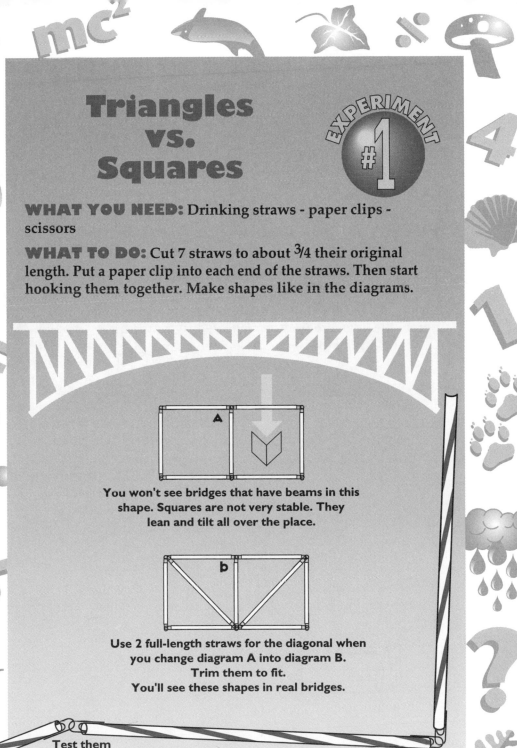

You won't see bridges that have beams in this shape. Squares are not very stable. They lean and tilt all over the place.

Use 2 full-length straws for the diagonal when you change diagram A into diagram B.
Trim them to fit.
You'll see these shapes in real bridges.

Test them for strength by holding their ends apart.
Do they sag in the middle?

An Eggsperiment

WHAT YOU NEED: 3 eggs - 6 plastic soda pop bottle caps - metal pie tin

WHAT TO DO: Make 3 little stands like the one in the drawing. Stand them together in a triangle-shape and put the pie tin on top. How much stuff can you put in the pie tin before the eggs break? *You Can* even try putting a heavy stone or a brick in the plate.

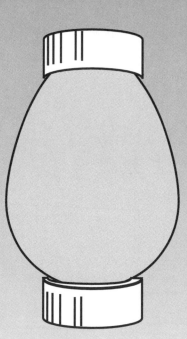

WHAT IS GOING ON:

Three eggs set up like this can easily support the weight of a brick. The ends of the eggshells are arches. You'll see that shape in bridges a lot, too. It's a very strong shape. Many bridges feature both triangles and arches.

P.S. from Jax: Suspension bridges, like the Golden Gate Bridge, use arches too. The shape of the long cables is an arch - an arch that is upside-down.

Dear Jax,

What are goose bumps? Where do they come from?

Callie Wilson
Columbus, Ohio

Dear Callie,

Talking about goose bumps means talking about something controversial (con-tra-VUR-shul). When something is controversial, people think different things about the same subject and talk about it a lot. So here goes.

We get goose bumps because of *evolution* (ev-eh-LU-shun). Evolution is a thing some people don't believe in. But many people - like me - do believe it. That makes it controversial.

Evolution is a theory that says living things change over time as their environments change.

Jax Place

Goose Bumps: Evolution in Action

Goose bumps are all about insulation and keeping warm. When fur is all fluffed up, it's a better insulator. It's better at keeping out the cold. Humans aren't covered with fur. But our prehistoric, prehuman ancestors probably were. This is the evolution part.

When it got cold, their fur stood on end, trapping air and forming an insulation barrier. Our goose bumps are sort of a leftover from those days - millions of years ago.

Cooling off

Staying warm

When it's hot, little muscles at each hair (1) relax. Your hair is relaxed. Your sweat glands (2) pump out body heat in sweat. Your blood vessels (3) get big to take more heat to the skin to get rid of it.

When it's cold, the arrector muscle (1) pulls the hair up. The duct to the sweat glands (2) gets small to conserve heat. Our blood vessels (3) get small to save heat. Hair standing up doesn't make good insulation anymore - we don't have enough fur for that. But it does make goose bumps (4).

Goose Bumps on Purpose

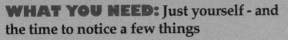

WHAT YOU NEED: Just yourself - and the time to notice a few things

WHAT TO DO: The next time you take a bath or a shower, pay closer attention to what's happening.

After the shower is off, or you're out of the tub, step into the center of the room. Don't grab a towel. Relax with your arms at your sides. Take a deep, deep breath. Let it *all out slowly*. What happened?

WHAT IS GOING ON: You just had a reflexive event. *Reflex* means it happens without you having to make it happen. The body reacts on its own. As you let out that deep breath, you relaxed and gave up some muscle control. You probably had a big shiver.

Your muscles shivered on their own. The reason for the muscles doing that is to *make more body heat*. Believe it or not, your goose bumps are also about getting warm.

P.S. from Beakman: Cold is not the only thing that can cause our hair to stand on end. Fear or anger can cause the same reflex. The same is true for other mammals. You'll notice that on a cat or dog.

Dear Jax,

How is mayonnaise made?

Mary-Frances Bartels Denver, Colorado

Dear Mary-Frances,

People love their mayonnaise so much they seem to put it on everything - even corned beef.

Mayonnaise is truly a miracle of the material world. It's something that shouldn't be able to happen, but does! Oil and water *do* mix in mayonnaise!

Mayo is a thick mixture of oil and vinegar. (Vinegar is mostly water.) But try to mix those 2 things together, and they always separate. Yet right there on your halftime-show sandwich they do mix! We call that kind of mixture an emulsion (ee-MUL-shun).

Jax Place
Jax Place

The Mayo Clinic

WHAT YOU NEED: 2 egg yolks - 1 teaspoon salt - 1 tablespoon vinegar - 1 cup vegetable (or olive) oil - family help or permission - blender *Optional: lecithin powder (from health food store)*

WHAT TO DO: Take the center out of the blender lid. Put the egg yolks into the blender with the salt and vinegar and whip until it's light and fluffy. Add the oil *drop by drop* while the yolks are still being beaten. This takes *a lot* of time. Do not be in a hurry or the oil globs will touch each other and the mayonnaise will turn into mayo-soup. When the mayo gets thick, stop adding oil.

SO WHAT: If your eggs aren't fresh, you'll end up with mayo-soup. If that starts to happen, immediately add a pinch of lecithin powder. That will turn the mayo-soup back into mayonnaise.

If your mayo doesn't get thick, try again with fresh eggs and with more patience, adding the oil much slower. Or add less oil.

Mayonnaise takes practice. But then again, you are making something that shouldn't even exist, and that can be difficult.

ITZA MIRACLE
MAYONNAISE

113

The Science of Mayonnaise

oiL

viNegar

Oil and vinegar don't mix. They pull away from each other. They touch each other as little as possible, in as small a common area as possible. That's why there are layers. Try mixing them!

In an emulsion, the oil is broken up into teeny-weeny globs that can't be allowed to touch each other. If they were to touch, they would join each other and keep joining until we get layers again.

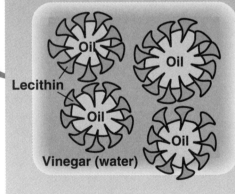

Lecithin

Oil

Oil

Oil

Oil

Vinegar (water)

The thing we use to keep the globules of oil from touching each other is called an emulsifier (ee-MUL-sa-fi-ur). In mayonnaise, the emulsifier is lecithin (LESS-a-thin) - a chemical found in fresh egg yolks. If the eggs aren't fresh, there's a lot less lecithin, and you get mayo-*soup*, not mayonnaise.

P.S. from Beakman: If you happen to have the TV on while you're making mayo, people may start yelling about the TV's picture. The sparks in the blender motor generate radio waves that make *visual noise* on the TV screen.

Dear Beakman,

How can a ship made of metal float? Steel and iron sink. But boats made out of them do not. Why?

**Earl Mills
Corpus Christi,
Texas**

Dear Earl,

It is a little hard to understand why steel or iron can be made into big ships. Yes, a chunk of steel is heavy and will sink in water. But steel is not as heavy as the water that the ships' hull pushes away, or displaces.

Here are the experiments *You Can* do to learn how they make boats out of steel that float.

Beakman

Beakman Place

Pushing Water Away: Displacement

WHAT YOU NEED: Big jar or bowl - soda bottle - water - marking pen

WHAT TO DO: Fill the jar half-full of water. Make a mark on the jar where the top of the water is. Fill the soda bottle half-full of water and mark it, too. Push the soda bottle down into the jar. Push down until the top of the water in the bottle meets the top of the water in the jar. Look at the marks you made. See if they still match the top of the water in both the soda bottle and the big jar.

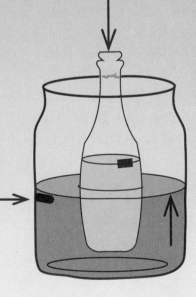

WHAT IS GOING ON: Your soda bottle pushed away the water in the big jar. That is why the water line moved up. The water in the soda bottle stayed the same. Feel how heavy the soda bottle and its water are. Anything the same size that weighs less will float. Anything heavier will sink.

Floating

WHAT YOU NEED: Bucket - aluminum foil - water - hammer

WHAT TO DO: Fill the bucket with water. Make a little boat with the foil and put it on the water. What happened? Take the foil out of the water and make it into a little ball. Then take it outside to a sidewalk and hammer the ball until you cannot make it any smaller. Fold it over and hammer it more. Put the little foil ball in the water. What happens?

WHAT IS GOING ON:

The little boat floated. That is because it was not as heavy as the water it pushed away. Then you made the foil smaller and it could not push away enough water to float. The ball weighed exactly the same as the boat. But it got so small it was heavier than the water it could push away. So it sank.

Even though a ship is very big and very very heavy, it is not as heavy as the water it pushes away. That is why a big ship made of steel can float! (Don't forget to use the water from your experiments for the plants outside.)

If you live near a lake or river, visit the docks to see the boats. Some boats are made of concrete, which is heavy. The cement boats float because they weigh less than the water they push away.

In most libraries books about boats have the number 478.30. Check it out!

Dear Beakman,

How do fiber optics work?

Justin Kuo
Lexington, Kentucky

Dear Justin,

Fiber optics is a term we hear a lot these days. Sometimes the talk is just *hype* - a way of selling something by getting everyone all excited.

Fiber optics is pretty much just a new kind of cable. A regular cable sends electricity into a wire circuit. The fiber optic cable sends pure laser light into a thin strand of glass. The big difference is *You Can* send lots more stuff with fiber optics.

Beakman

Beakman Place

Fiber Optics at Home

EXPERIMENT #1

WHAT YOU NEED: Small jar with lid - long black sock - flashlight - the kitchen sink - nail - hammer - *total* darkness - grown-up help

WHAT TO DO: Punch 2 holes in the lid of the jar. Put the flashlight all the way into the bottom of the sock. Fill the jar with water and put the lid on. Slide the jar into the sock.

Turn off the lights. Turn on the flashlight. Now pour the water into your sink.

SO WHAT: Light travels in *straight* lines. That means your experiment should shine light along the line marked A. But it doesn't. Your light shone along line B.

You just bent a beam of light around a corner. This is exactly how we can use laser light to send telephone calls down a long, curvy fiber of glass. Inside strands of glass (and in streams of water) the light bounces off the *inside* walls. No matter which way the strand or stream bends, the light will follow it, bouncing along inside.

We can send lots of stuff through a fiber optic cable - way, way more than we can send through regular wire cable. Look at this drawing and *You Can* see that we can send different colored light through the same fiber optic cable.

Phone calls
Newspapers
TV

You *already* get phone calls that were sent in part on fiber optic cable.

The hype is about what kinds of things we *might* use it for - like newspapers on a computer or movies whenever we want or even more home shopping.

What turns hype into reality is whether or not people are willing to pay money for all this stuff that *might* be.

P.S. from Beakman: Laser light is special because its light waves are in sync with each other. That means the light will not spread out like other light and can focus lots of energy tightly.

Dear Beakman,

How does a phonograph record work?

**Kenny Kangas
Maple Grove,
Minnesota**

Dear Kenny,

The word itself explains a lot about phono-graphs. Phono means *sound*. And graphic means *written*. Phonographic means *written with sound*. A record is covered with grooves written by sounds. Our record players read that sound-writing. Back in olden times, in the 1960s, before cassettes and CDs, records and records on radio were the only ways for music to be shared on a mass scale. Records were so important to culture, words about them became slang words - like groovy. Ask your family and grandparents for other words.

Beakman

Beakman Place

121

Milli Vanilli
&
Marcel Marceau

Good Vibrations
Get in the Groove

WHAT YOU NEED: A plastic soda bottle - scissors - balloon

WHAT TO DO: ⚠ Cut the bottom of the bottle away. Cut the very end of the balloon off, the end you blow up. Now stretch the top of the balloon over the top of the bottle. Pull it down so the balloon is tight. Pick up the bottle and hold the open end right up to your mouth. Hold a finger very lightly on the tight balloon. Start talking or yelling into the bottle.

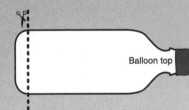

Balloon top

Say the word *vibration* or *groovy*. What's happening at the other end under your finger?

WHAT IS GOING ON: The balloon buzzed under your fingers. It was vibrating. The sound waves from your yelling made the balloon shiver. If you could attach a pencil to the balloon, you would be able to draw a wavy line just with the sound of your voice. The pencil would shiver, too. A record groove is a long wavy line made by a vibrating cutting needle at the record factory. That needle behaves just like the pencil would - it vibrates and writes a wavy line.

Make a Phonograph

WHAT YOU NEED: Piece of paper - pin - old phonograph record - turntable from your stereo

WHAT TO DO: Make a cone with the paper. Use some tape to make sure the cone doesn't open at the side. Go outside and lightly scrape the pin on the sidewalk a few times. This will dull the point a bit. Stick it through the end of the cone. This is your record player. In fact, it's a lot like the first phonographs ever made.

Playing a record with a pin will cut away some of the groove and wreck the record. So, find an old record that no one cares about, something like Tony Orlando and Dawn. Don't use a family favorite.

Put the record on the turntable and turn it on. Hold the cone from the large end and gently place the pin on the record. What happened?

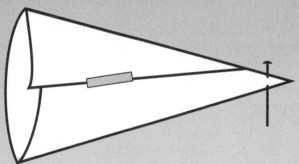

WHAT IS GOING ON: You just made a Victrola – an old-fashioned record player that didn't use electricity. The wavy grooves in your record made the pin vibrate. The cone made the vibrations louder. Those vibrations are the music.

The first phonograph used cylinders, not disks. It was invented by Thomas Alva Edison. The first words ever recorded were Mr. Edison reading "Mary Had a Little Lamb."

123

Dear Rebecca,

To talk about this subject, we have to use a word that isn't polite. We'll use it anyway so that everyone knows what is being discussed. The word is snot. The polite way of saying it is mucus (MUKE-us). But even that word can be used impolitely. Polite or impolite is more a matter of your intentions.

Snot is thick and sticks to just about everything. It's a good thing, too, because mucus is a barrier against germs. It helps keep them outside. It also cuts off a very important part of the way we taste food.

Beakman

Beakman Place

Tastes and Smells

WHAT YOU NEED: A sugar bowl

WHAT TO DO: Wet your finger and dab it into the sugar. Stick your tongue way out and touch the sugar on the very back of your tongue. Don't close your mouth. With your tongue still out, try to taste the sugar. Now touch the sugar to the tip of your tongue.

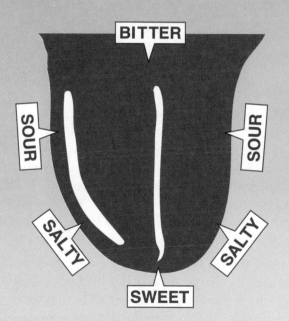

BITTER

SOUR

SOUR

SALTY

SALTY

SWEET

WHAT IS GOING ON: You can't taste sweet on the back of your tongue. Your tongue can taste only 4 different flavors and does it on different parts. We need our sense of smell to give food its full flavor.

You do Experiment #1 every time you lick an ice-cream cone. You taste the sweet as you lick the ice cream with the tip of your tongue. The other flavors come from our sense of smell.

125

The Nose Knows

WHAT YOU NEED: 3 different flavors of a drink mix like Kool-Aid™ - a friend - a blindfold - 4 glasses

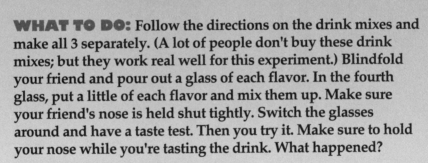

WHAT TO DO: Follow the directions on the drink mixes and make all 3 separately. (A lot of people don't buy these drink mixes; but they work real well for this experiment.) Blindfold your friend and pour out a glass of each flavor. In the fourth glass, put a little of each flavor and mix them up. Make sure your friend's nose is held shut tightly. Switch the glasses around and have a taste test. Then you try it. Make sure to hold your nose while you're tasting the drink. What happened?

WHAT IS GOING ON:
When you have a cold, your body is working overtime trying to keep out germs. Several openings in our bodies are protected by mucus. It's a barrier that keeps all that stuff outside. Germs get stuck in the sticky gunk. The problem is we can't smell because our nose is full of snot. That means we can't taste very many flavors. When you held your nose, your drinks had only one taste - sweet. And if you think about it, these drinks don't really taste like what they're called anyway. No real grape tastes anything like a grape drink.

Dear Beakman,

Why is a knife sharp?

**Katie Krause
Staples,
Minnesota**

Dear Katie,

Knives provide many challenges. First there's the weird way you spell their name. Then there are the dangers. After all, the whole idea of a knife is to cut things. And you do not want to cut yourself.

Knives are about force and concentrating force. The reason a knife is sharp is that a very fine point concentrates force - enough force to slice things apart.

The opposite of how a knife works is a bed of nails. It has nothing to do with being in a trance. It does have to do with spreading the force out.

Beakman

Beakman Place

Concentrating the Force

EXPERIMENT #1

WHAT YOU NEED: Cereal boxtop - stick of butter or margarine

WHAT TO DO: Lay the boxtop flat on the butter. Now push down. Next, stand the boxtop on its edge and push down. What happened?

WHAT IS GOING ON: The flat boxtop would not cut into the butter. Your force down was spread out over the whole width of the boxtop. On its edge, the boxtop concentrated your force and sliced the butter. The smaller the edge, the more it concentrates the same force.

Chocolate Frosted SUGAR BOMBS

KNIFE NOTICE

⚠ Warning: Knives are *extremely dangerous*. The idea here is to explain them only. Never touch a knife without family permission.

Spreading Force Out

EXPERIMENT #2

WHAT YOU NEED: Balloon - straight pins - shoe box - graph paper - brick - permission and help from your family

WHAT TO DO: Tape down the graph paper on the bottom of the box. Stick 1 pin every place 2 lines cross. When you turn the box over, it should be full of pins sticking straight up. Blow up the balloon and place it in the box on the pins. Balance the brick on the balloon.

WHAT IS GOING ON:

The force of the brick was spread out over dozens and dozens of pins. There wasn't enough pressure on any one pin to burst the balloon. This is a safe model of the bed-of-nails trick that people can get all mystical about.

YOU CAN

P.S. from Jax: Concentration of force is why high-heeled shoes sink into soft dirt. All the weight is concentrated on those teeny little heels.

Dear Beakman,

How do you make a solar oven?

**Elliot Harlan
Centerville,
Indiana**

Dear Elliot,

Building a solar oven is a family project. First, because it's all about building and it's better to figure out and build together.

Second, you'll have to buy stuff, and that involves selling your family on a trip to the hardware store.

Third, ovens get very hot (400°), and the glass in your oven can be dangerous.

Beakman

Beakman Place

Build with Beakman- Solar Oven

WHAT YOU NEED: Help from your family - a sunny day - cardboard boxes

SHOPPING LIST: Foam ice chest - piece of glass about 8" wider than the width of the ice chest - lots of aluminum foil - duct tape - safety/work gloves - refrigerated bread dough or dinner rolls - oven thermometer

WHAT TO DO: Ask a grown-up to use a bread knife to cut the ice chest like the drawing. Ask him or her to tape the edges of the glass. Line the chest with foil. Cut up the cardboard into 4 trapezoidal shapes. Discuss that last word with your family. Cover those shapes with foil and mount them onto the glass to make the oven's lid. Use lots of duct tape. This is a *trial and effort* thing. Work with and talk to your family about what that means. ⚠ *Be very careful with the fragile glass!*

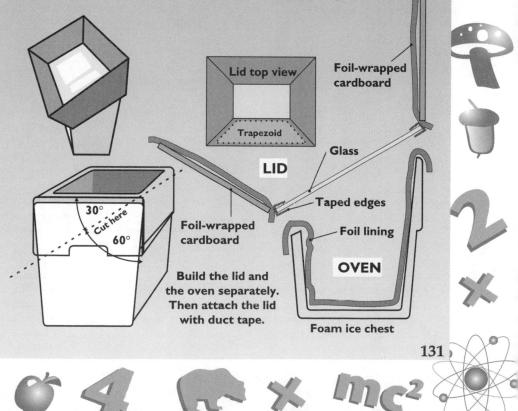

Lid top view
Foil-wrapped cardboard
Trapezoid
LID
Glass
Foil-wrapped cardboard
Taped edges
Foil lining
30°
Cut here
60°
OVEN

Build the lid and the oven separately. Then attach the lid with duct tape.

Foam ice chest

MORE STUFF: Decide which way to lay the oven and point it toward the sun. Put in the bread dough and the thermometer and attach the lid using duct tape.

In about a hour, your thermometer could be reading 350° to 400°. Watch the bread to check on its color. The cooking time on the package won't work. Your oven takes a lot longer to heat up.

When the bread is done, ask a grown-up wearing gloves to open the oven. ⚠ *The glass lid will be dangerously hot!*

If the sun is high in the sky, stand the oven up, like drawing A. If it's low in the sky, lay it on its side like drawing B.

A

B

P.S. from Jax: Your oven also demonstrates what the Greenhouse Effect means. The glass in your oven traps heat in the oven the same way that carbon dioxide in our air traps heat on planet Earth.

Dear Jax,

Why is poop brown?

Crystal Goodins
Davenport, Iowa

Dear Crystal,

Every living thing on this planet produces waste. Everything! So it's not like anyone can pretend not to be interested in the answer to your question.

The answer is way interesting. It's all about bacteria and chemicals and your good health.

Jax Place

What Is This . . . Stuff? Anyway?

Stuff happens. In fact it happens all the time. Your body is always going through cycles - routines - all the time. One of them is the creation, use and reuse of blood cells.

After your body is done using a blood cell, it will die and a new blood cell will replace it. Your body will take apart the old blood cell and use the chemicals in it to do more work. It will also throw out the stuff it's done using. A chemical called bilirubin (bill-e-ROO-bin) is made when your body takes old blood cells apart. And bilirubin is brown. That's where the brown comes from.

When your body is done with these red blood cells, it takes them apart. A brown chemical is one of the things that's left over.

Our Old Friends: Intestinal Bacteria

See if you have a soup can in your kitchen. Use it to think about the weight and mass of something inside of you.

Solid waste is made from food that you've used. You took as many nutrients as you could from it. That's what digestion (di-GES-chun) is. The waste also contains water; stuff your body is done using and is getting rid of, like old cells; and bacteria. Good bacteria.

You have about a half a soup can of bacteria inside your guts all the time.

They help you digest food. Hard-to-digest foods - like beans - are a thick paste by the time they get to your intestines - where bacteria finish digesting them for you. You couldn't digest them very well without bacteria.

If you don't include the water, $1/3$ of your solid body waste is bacteria.

Compare this drawing up close to how it looks from across the room.

Dear Jax,

Why does the TV go fuzzy when the electric mixer is on?

**Michelle Bordeaux
Winnipeg, Manitoba**

Dear Michelle,

Television is really radio waves carrying both sound and pictures. Radio waves are carefully controlled electromagnetic radiation.

The electric motor in your mixer makes lots and lots of electric sparks as it spins. And all sparks make electromagnetic radiation. Sometimes we call this radiation RF, which stands for *radio frequency*.

Your TV picks up the RF from the TV station and also the RF from the mixer. The mixer's RF is not controlled and is all mixed up. That's what messes up your TV.

Jax Place
Jax Place

Get Some Sparks Going

EXPERIMENT #1

WHAT YOU NEED: Small appliances with motors and permission to use them - AM radio

WHAT TO DO: Tune the radio to what I call *Zen radio*. I mean, tune so that you can't hear any station clearly. Tune to *no station*. Turn on the appliances one by one; change their speeds; turn them on in groups. Listen to the sounds the radio makes.

SO WHAT:

You heard lots of rapid clicking, and the speed of the clicks changed as the speed of the motors changed. If you look in the vent holes of some appliances, you can even see sparking as it happens.

The invention of the radio happened after people began paying attention to sparks and what they do. This means your Mixmaster is really a little, out-of-control radio station!

If you invent a code, *You Can* send messages to your friends on Zen radio with an appliance.

The sparks inside this mixer make wild and crazy radio waves - RF - so crazy that the TV picture will roll and be crazy itself. The noise you'll hear in your experiment is turned into a picture on TV. That's what is meant by the term *noisy image*.

P.S. from Beakman: The word radiation can sometimes confuse you. Radiation means when something radiates from one location outward - like light from a lightbulb. Not all radiation is unsafe. The dangerous kind is called ionizing radiation.

Dear Beakman,

What is the International Date Line?

D.R. Wagner
Sacramento, California

Dear D.R.,

One of the ways we keep track of time is the spin of the Earth. That means the Earth is like an enormous clock. The Sun overhead is like the clock's hand. Wherever the Sun is straight up, it's noon. On the other side of the planet from noontime, it's midnight. And midnight is when we change days and begin tomorrow.

That means tomorrow moves around the planet as the planet spins. But the next date has to start somewhere. That's what the International Date Line is - the place tomorrow begins! It's not a real line. It's just a place all Earthlings agree on. We all agree that tomorrow will begin there.

Beakman
Beakman Place

139

Like Spokes in a Wheel

EXPERIMENT #1

WHAT YOU NEED: This book - scissors - thumbtack - take a trip to the photocopier

WHAT TO DO: Photocopy the picture of Earth below at the same size as shown and cut it out. Use the tack to attach it to the dot in the center of the large diagram. Spin Earth in the direction of the arrow.

SO WHAT: The drawing is what the Earth below looks like from above the North Pole. The lines are the time zones. There are 24 of them because there are 24 hours in a day. Because there's always a midnight somewhere on the Earth, it's already tomorrow someplace on the planet. The IDL is the place that new day began.

IDL

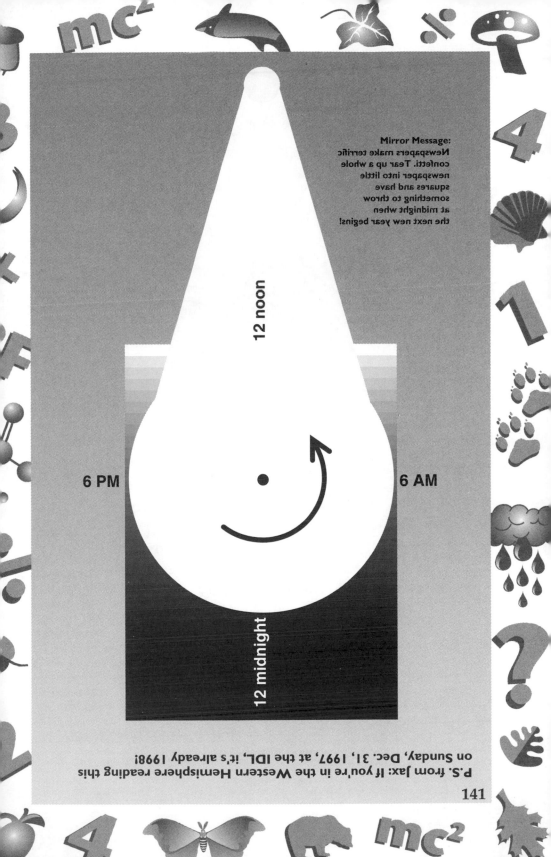

Mirror Message:
Newspapers make terrific
confetti. Tear up a whole
newspaper into little
squares and have
something to throw
at midnight when
the next new year begins!

12 noon

6 PM

6 AM

12 midnight

P.S. from Jax: If you're in the Western Hemisphere reading this on Sunday, Dec. 31, 1997, at the IDL, it's already 1998!

Dear Beakman,

Which way is down?

Jason Lacey
Minnetonka,
Minnesota

Dear Jason,

The answer depends on where you are. That's because the Earth is nearly spherical. A sphere (SFEAR) is like a ball. The way down in Minnetonka, Minnesota, is the way up off the western coast of Australia. And there is a special place where the rules change. At the exact center of the planet, every direction is straight up. Confused? *You Can* do these experiments to clear things up.

Beakman

Beakman Place

Thinking Globally

WHAT YOU NEED: Pencil - orange

WHAT TO DO: Think of the stem as the North Pole of the Earth. Ask someone to show you where on the planet you live. Or look at a globe. Stick the pencil in the orange at that place and aim for the center. That's the way down from where you live. Keep pushing and see where it comes out. Take out the pencil and drop the orange on the floor.

WHAT IS GOING ON: Even though it looks flat, the Earth is shaped like a ball - or an orange. That means there is an infinite number of ways down. When you dropped the orange, it went down - straight toward the center of the Earth. But that direction was only for you and the place you're at.

Down is a different direction for every spot on Earth. To demonstrate that the Earth is like a ball, just look at the view. You can't see past the horizon. That's because the Earth is curving down away from your point of view. If the Earth was flat, you could see from Minnesota to Australia.

Looking Locally

WHAT YOU NEED:
The orange from Experiment #1

WHAT TO DO: Ask someone who knows about knives to slice the orange in half. ⚠ (Do not do this yourself if you're not allowed to use a kitchen knife. They can be dangerous.) Look inside and use your powers of imagination. Think of the skin as the surface of Earth. Put yourself on a spot. Ask yourself, which way is down? The answer is the direction that's toward the center of the orange. Now put yourself on a different part of the orange. Did the way down change? Imagine you're at the center of the orange. Every way toward the skin would be the way up.

If you're here, the way down is like this:

Both arrows point toward the way down.

But if you're here, the way down is different.

If you think this is strange, it gets more weird when you think about the universe. On the planet Mars, down is toward the center of that planet - not toward our planet's center. In outer space, where there is no gravity, there is no down and no up at all.

144

Dear Jax,
Why do you get all dirty when you read a newspaper?

Voula Zerzakos
London, Ontario

Dear Voula,

Ask any newspaper editor, and he or she will tell you newspapers are not dirty.

The color in ink is called the pigment, and the pigment is carried in a liquid. In newspaper ink, the liquid is a kind of oil.

The natural oils in your skin can also carry the pigment. When you brush most newspapers with your finger, you'll pick up black pigment. *You Can* also pick up the ink with a terrific plastic slime that *You Can* make!

Jax Place

145

Make Some News Glue

WHAT YOU NEED:

White glue - borax (from the soap section of the supermarket) - water - plastic film canister - covered jar - spoons - measuring cup - help and permission from a grown-up in your family

WHAT TO DO: Add 1 level teaspoon of borax to ½ cup of warm water in your jar. Close the lid and shake until it's dissolved. Clean and dry the cup. In the measuring cup, add 2 teaspoons water to 2 teaspoons white glue. Mix really well. Add 1 teaspoon of your borax solution. Keep mixing and poking the blob of putty for 3 to 5 minutes. Let this sit in your cup for a full 5 minutes. Pick up and squeeze into a ball.

Your slime will look especially good when you lift off color comics! When it gets all gross and full of ink, make more!

You can spread your news glue into a flat blob on top of a newspaper. When you lift it off, you'll pull ink off with it.

Save your slime in the film canister. That keeps it from drying out. Use the borax solution to make more slime. If you do not, *throw the borax solution away!* Do not eat or drink anything in this experiment!

P.S. from Beakman: Your news glue-slime-putty junk is made out of the plastic polymers that are a part of white glue.

Dear Sara,

To make a napkin *You Can* use any soft and absorbent paper. *You Can* also make a napkin with a piece of cloth.

To make a napkin *pretty*, you have to use more - a lot more. You have to use *geometry*.

Every once in a while, some sexist bozo will say that girls don't do well at geometry - the math of shapes. Well, I don't think that's true.

I think any girl (or boy) who can turn a limp Scotties into a dazzling dish-top display has geometry mastered - and has a real flair for entertaining as well.

Jax Place
Jax Place

The Crowning Touch

WHAT YOU NEED: Paper or cloth napkin - a little patience

WHAT TO DO: Follow this procedure. When you get it, fold several and stand them up on plates for dinner tonight.

1

Start with a square. A square has 4 sides that are all the same length and 4 corners that are 90 degrees each. If you're using a paper napkin, start by opening it up to give you a big square to work with.

2

Fold the square in half. That gives you a rectangle - 4 90-degree corners and sides that are not all the same.

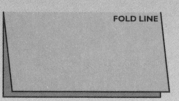

FOLD LINE

3

Fold the top corner down and the opposing corner up. That makes a parallelogram, which is the shape in drawing #4. It's like a rectangle relaxing and leaning over.

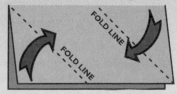

FOLD LINE
FOLD LINE

4

Turn the whole thing over and fold it in half along the dotted line. Let the peak of the triangle flip up so that it looks like drawing #5.

FOLD LINE

5

So now your napkin looks a little like 2 pyramids connected with a bridge. Fold in each side on the 2 dotted lines.

FOLD LINE   FOLD LINE

6

Tuck the end of the pyramid inside the flap you'll find on the other pyramid. Now, just stand it up and open the inside so that it looks like a crown.

This standing napkin has lots of shapes and is also a terrific way to impress visiting relatives. Make as many as *You Can.*

TUCK

Borrow them for free!
P.S. from Beakman: When you fold flat paper into the shapes of other things, you're doing the art of origami. There are books on origami (and on many different napkin folds) at your library.

Dear Beakman,

What makes the whistle-sound when you blow through your lips?

What changes the tones?

Elysa Chao
Cleveland, Ohio

Dear Elysa,

Your question turns out to be truly wonderful because the answer is not really understood.

Questions without answers are terrific because they're proof that there's stuff out there waiting to be discovered.

All whistles work pretty much the same way. Air is made to vibrate really quickly. Those vibrations are the whistling sound. *You Can* change the pitch of the sound by changing how much air you vibrate.

Beakman

Beakman Place

Edge-Tone

Flutes, soda-pop bottles and the coach's whistle make sound with edge-tones.

Air is blown across an edge that separates the air and causes little swirls called vortices.

If there is an air chamber above or below the swirls, air will be forced into it. It will pack as full of air as it can. Then, the air will escape out past the swirls. Then it will start over again and again.

This packing full/unpacking happens very quickly—hundreds of times a second. That's what the whistle sound is: the air vibrating, packing and unpacking.

Hole-Tone

Human beings and most teakettles whistle with hole-tones.

When air is forced through circular openings, it can swirl in doughnut shapes.

These doughnut swirls can vibrate air, too. This is the part that's not really understood about human whistling. No one seems to have discovered the details of the air flow. All we know is that air inside our mouth is resonating (REZ-on-ate-ing).

Make a Tuneful Whistle

WHAT YOU NEED: 2 soda bottles (make sure they're exactly alike)

WHAT TO DO: Hold 1 bottle up to your lips and blow across the top. Move the air flow with your upper lip until you get a whistle. Hold the other bottle up to your ear. Blow across the sounding bottle again. Try filling the ear bottle half full of water. Do the same with the sounding bottle.

WHAT IS GOING ON: The bottle at your ear resonated— it made the same whistle as the sounding bottle. When you added water, you changed the size of the air chamber. Water in the sounding bottle raised the pitch. Less air can vibrate faster, and faster vibrations are higher notes.

Water in the ear bottle made it quiet. The air chamber wasn't the same size as the sounding bottle anymore. When it's the same size, the air in the ear bottle is exactly the right size to be easily vibrated just by the sound of the whistle.

HEAR HERE

BLOW HERE

The edge of the bottle split the air flow and started packing and unpacking the bottle with air. That's what makes the whistle sound.

P.S. from Jax: When a pop bottle plays the note middle-C, the air inside the bottle packs and unpacks 256 times a second.

153

How does the human heart work?

Debra Judelson
Beverly Hills,
California

Dear Debra,

Thank you for your letter and the excellent question.

The human heart is a big set of muscles about the size of your fist. It's a pump that moves blood through miles of veins and arteries. That blood feeds all of the body's cells, removes cell waste and defends us against invaders like germs.

A pump is usually a machine with a set of pistons or a propeller-like set of blades. But the heart has none of those. It's basically a hollow, ball-like muscle.

You Can copy the pumping action of the heart in this experiment.

Beakman

Beakman Place

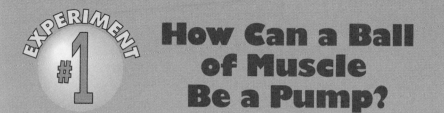

How Can a Ball of Muscle Be a Pump?

WHAT YOU NEED: An empty squeeze bottle with a closing top, like a dish-soap bottle

WHAT TO DO: The next time you take a bath, take a few minutes to turn your dish-soap bottle into a pump. Before you get in the tub, ask someone who's allowed to use a knife to cut a small hole in the bottom of the bottle.

You have to be able to cover the hole with your finger.

First, hold the bottle under water and fill it with water. Put the cap on and pull the top so that it's open. Hold one finger over the little hole and lift the top out of the water. The bottom of the bottle is still underwater. With the hole covered, squeeze the bottle.

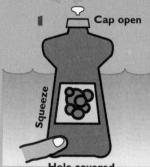

1
Cap open

Squeeze

Hole covered

Cap shut
2

Un-squeeze

Hole open

Keep squeezing the bottle and lift your finger off the hole. With the bottle still squeezed, shut the top of the cap. Now let the bottle expand. When it's full, cover the little hole with your finger again and open the cap.

Now you can start over again.

155

What Is Going On

Your squeeze bottle behaved a lot like the heart. It got bigger and smaller and sucked in and squeezed out bathwater. The heart does the same thing with blood.

Our hearts are divided into four chambers. Chambers A and B are called atriums (A-tree-umz). C and D are called ventricles (VEN-tree-culz). They squeeze and un-squeeze to pump blood.

Your experiment and your heart wouldn't work without valves. In your tub, the valves were your finger on the hole and the cap. In our heart, the valves are little flaps of muscle that open and close. In this simplified drawing, the valves have circles around them. The valves make sure that blood (or bathwater) goes in only one direction.

Dear Beakman,

Why do your fingers get all wrinkled in the bathtub?

Alex Curry
Marinwood, California

Dear Alex,

Your skin is what keeps you in. All the wet messy stuff we are on the inside is kept neat and protected by this bag of watertight stuff we call skin.

Your skin can absorb a lot of water, like a sponge. When it's holding water, your skin swells up a bit.

The skin on your fingertips and toes is thicker and swells up more - so much more that we get wrinkles. *You Can* use a potato to see it happen at a bigger size.

Beakman
Beakman Place

Our Skin Is a Sponge?

WHAT YOU NEED: Potato - butter knife - plastic bag - bowl of water - help from a grown-up - patience

WHAT TO DO: Make potato slices about $3/4$-inch thick. Cut a slice into 2 pieces like in the drawing. (Stick the butter knife in and out of the potato slice. Don't try turning the blade while you're cutting.) The 2 pieces should slide into each other and fit perfectly.

Seal 1 slice in the bag after you squeeze out the air. Put the other slice into a bowl of water for 3 or 4 hours. Do they still slide into each other and fit perfectly? Probably not.

Put this slice into the water   **Put this slice into the bag.**

A Giant Potato Takes a Bath

Your skin does the same thing a soaked potato does. It swells up as it absorbs water.

P.S. from Jax: The stuff You Can scratch off your fingers when they're all puckered is dead skin cells. The outside of our skin is all dead cells. When they get soaked, they're easier to remove.

Dear Jax,

What is in helium that makes it float?

Maryama Tagoe
Alexandria,
Virginia

Dear Maryama,

There's nothing in helium that makes it float. There is just helium in helium.

Helium is a pure element. That means it's made out of helium alone, and is not a bunch of other stuff mixed together.

The reason helium balloons float is that helium weighs less than the air we live in. We say that helium is *less dense* than the air. *You Can* look at density with a quick look around your kitchen.

Jax Place

Salad or Science?

WHAT YOU NEED: Cooking oil - vinegar - black pepper - as many spices as you like or can think of, like basil leaf or rosemary - jar with lid

WHAT TO DO: Mix equal amounts of the oil and vinegar in the jar. Dump in a lot of pepper and pinch in bits of the spices. Put on the lid and shake it up really well.

Wait until the oil and vinegar have formed 2 separate layers. Examine the place where the layers meet very closely. Look at what is floating. Look at *where* it is floating in the jar.

Add some greens and you've got lunch!

So What: Some of the spices sank to the bottom of the bottle. Some floated on the top. And some floated right in the middle on top of the vinegar and on the bottom of the oil.

That stuff in the middle is worth thinking about here.

It is less dense than the vinegar. These chunks weigh less than a same-sized *chunk* of vinegar would weigh. The vinegar pushes them up to the top. But they are heavier - more dense - than oil, so they cannot float in oil.

A helium balloon floats in air. It weighs less than an equalized *chunk* of air and the air pushes the balloon up like a cork floating in water.

But that same helium balloon would not float if you held it up in, say, hydrogen gas instead of air. That's because helium is heavier than hydrogen and it would sink.

YOU CAN

P.S. from Beakman: Vinegar and oil will always separate and will not mix. A third ingredient will help them kind of live together. Beaten egg turns vinegar and oil into mayonnaise!

Dear Jax,

How do levers make you stronger?

Eric Barther
Tel Aviv,
Israel

Dear Eric,

Levers do not make you stronger. A lever helps you do more work with the strength you already have. They work so well, *You Can* lift a whole car with just one hand - if you have the right lever.

A lever is a basic machine. All tools are combinations of the basic machines. Basic machines are things like: a wheel, a screw, an incline, a pulley or a lever.

Levers are all over your house. And *You Can* see how they work with these experiments.

Jax Place
Jax Place

Levers
(Lee-vurz or Lev-urz?)

The fulcrum (FULL-krum) is the place a lever rocks back and forth. You could call it a pivot.

When it's right in the middle of the lever, the amount of work you push down equals exactly the amount of load you can lift with the other end.

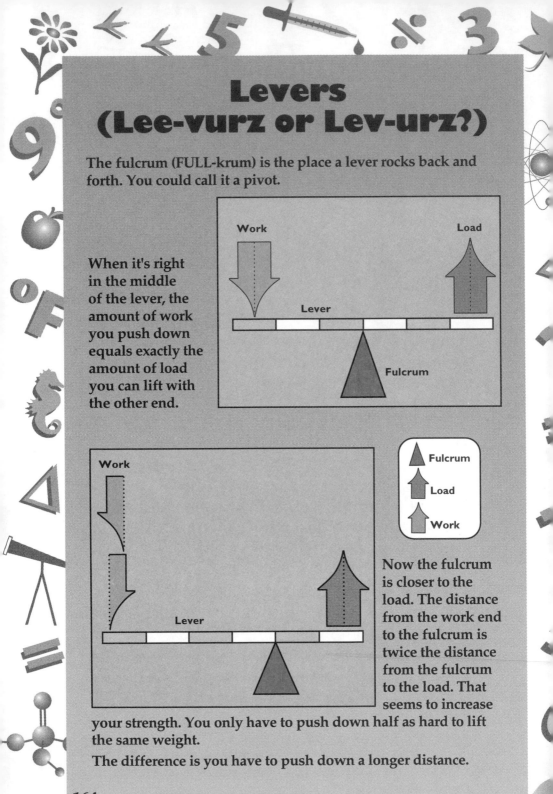

Now the fulcrum is closer to the load. The distance from the work end to the fulcrum is twice the distance from the fulcrum to the load. That seems to increase your strength. You only have to push down half as hard to lift the same weight.

The difference is you have to push down a longer distance.

Putting Levers to Work

EXPERIMENT #1

Pound a nail almost all the way into some wood. Use your fingers to pull it out. Now try pulling it out with the hammer. It's a lot easier. The claw on a hammer is a lever. We call this kind of lever a first-class lever. It does not mean it's a better lever - just that it's the first *kind* of lever.

EXPERIMENT #2

Use your first finger and thumb to pop off a metal cap from a soda bottle. Don't twist it off, pry it off. Now try a bottle opener. Much easier, right? A bottle opener is a second-class lever, which means the fulcrum is at the end of the lever and the load is in the middle.

P.S. from Beakman: *You Can lift a car with a jack*, which is a first-class lever. Other levers include nail clippers, wheelbarrows, baseball bats, pliers, scissors and lots more.

EXPERIMENT #3

A third-class lever has its fulcrum at one end and the load at the other end, with the work you do in the middle. It's how a fishing pole works. You lift just a short distance at the handle, but the end of the pole pops up several feet - hopefully with dinner on the line.

165

Dear Jonathan,

Most people do not get a headache from fluorescent light. Very few people do. Those few seem to be sensitive to all the blinking.

Fluorescent lights blink off and on 60 times every single second.

You Can see the blinking by using a special tool.

Beakman
Beakman Place

Faster Than the Eye Can See

WHAT YOU NEED: Electric mixer - help from a grown-up or permission to use it - fluorescent light - cardboard - tape - scissors

WHAT TO DO: Look at the drawing of the mixer and use it as a guide to building the spinning disk. Use only 1 of the mixer's beaters!

Use the back of a box to cut as large a circle as *You Can*. Use a dinner plate to help you draw the circle. Cut a hole in the center of it and one slot, as in the drawing. Slip the skinny end of 1 beater through the hole. Tape from underneath through the beater's fins to hold it on.

Turn on the fluorescent light. Hold your customized mixer at the end of your arm and turn it on. Look through the spinning disk at the fluorescent light. Change the mixer's speed.

Notice what happens to the light coming through the slot. Compare it to how a regular lightbulb or the TV looks.

Electricity in the United States is 120 volts A.C. That means *alternating current*. The energy flows in one direction and then turns around and flows in the other. It changes directions 60 times a second, which means it turns on and off 120 times a second.

Tape

SO WHAT:

You just built a kind of stroboscope (STROB-oh-skohp). As the speed changed, you saw spokes of light. The spinning slot acted to slow down the blinking. You could also see orange light in the dark bands in between the spokes. That's the color the light makes as it turns off.

P.S. from Jax: Your stroboscope is a lot like a tool a mechanic uses to tune up your car - a timing light. You *can* find one at a house in your neighborhood that has car parts on the front lawn.

Dear Beakman,

Why does a soda straw look bent in a glass of water?

Peter Bochenski
Oshawa, Ontario

Dear Peter,

You Can affect light and light beams several different ways. *You Can* bounce them, which is also called reflection. And *You Can* bend them, which is called refraction (re-FRAK-shun). Refraction is what happens with lenses of all kinds, from camera lenses to eyeglasses. It's also what's happening when you look through a glass of water at a straw.

There are lots of experiments *You Can* do to bend light. These 2 are my favorites. Find more at your library.

Beakman

Beakman Place

Water Is a Lens

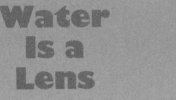

EXPERIMENT #1

WHAT YOU NEED:

Clear jar - water - shoe box - flashlight

WHAT TO DO: Cut two slits in one end of the box like in the drawing. At night, when it's very dark, put a jar of water in the box. Shine your flashlight through the slits. Watch what happens to the light beams.

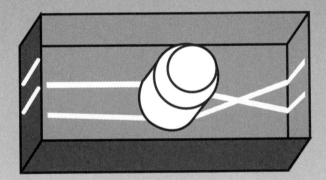

WHAT IS GOING ON:

The water bends the beams of light and they will criss-cross. If you put a magnifying glass or a lens in the box, the same thing will happen to the light. Water acts like a lens and bends – or refracts – light.

The next time you see a pond or a stream, look at the bottom through the water. The water will bend the light and make the bottom look much closer to you than it really is. Other liquids and even air also bend light. That's in Experiment #2.

Rates of Refraction

WHAT YOU NEED: Empty glass jar - water - rubbing alcohol - cooking oil - ruler - help and permission from your family ⚠ (Alcohol is dangerous.)

WHAT TO DO: Put about 2 inches of water in the jar. Tilt it to one side and gently pour in the same amount of oil. Tilt it back up. Now tilt it over again and gently add the rubbing alcohol. Pour slowly. When you straighten the jar, you'll see 3 separate layers. Stick in a ruler and look at it from the side. What happens?

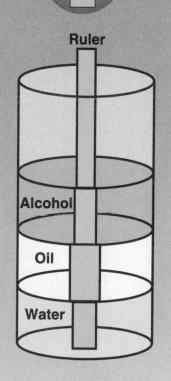

Ruler

Alcohol

Oil

Water

WHAT IS GOING ON: The ruler was all different sizes. The oil bends light the most, and the ruler looked very big. Water bends light less, and the ruler wasn't enlarged as much. Alcohol enlarged the ruler some, but not as much as water.

You Can also bend light at the same time you reflect it. Look into a shiny spoon. You'll see yourself upside down. The light criss-crossed and flipped your face upside down.

Why and how do people make toys?

Tolulope
Omokaiye
Chicago, Illinois

Dear Tolulope,

People make toys so that we can use our imaginations and take a trip to worlds that we make up for ourselves. In these new worlds it's *not* just a tiny tin truck. It's a huge gravel truck in which we're hauling enormous boulders.

When we play, it's *not* just a computer game. It is the real thing, and lives are at stake! Play is fun and teaches us stuff. Play is good. It gives your imagination room to move.

Anyone can make a toy. Really. You too, Tolulope. Toys are made of just about anything *You Can* have fun with. Even a newspaper can be a toy.

Jax Place
Jax Place

Tools, Toys & Tons of Fun

ATT AGAIN!
GOOD & EVIL

Newspaper

Toothpick

Lay the toothpick diagonally across a corner.
Then roll it up really tight.

WHAT YOU NEED: Newspaper - toothpicks - tape - scissors

WHAT TO DO: Unfold a single large piece of newspaper. Lay a toothpick across 1 corner and carefully roll up the newspaper. Do it very tightly and then tape it closed. After you've rolled up 18 of these, trim off the ends so all 18 are the same length. You might want to make more than 18. You'll need 70 or so to build a skyscraper to the ceiling.

SO WHAT: So now you've got these sticks that are about $2\frac{1}{2}$ feet long. They're pretty sturdy, too. So how about building something like a skyscraper with them? It can be tall enough to reach the ceiling in your house.

Get ahold of a roll of masking tape and pretend you're the supervisor and crew of a huge construction job in Chicago's Loop - which is what people in Chicago call their downtown.

173

Think Big

1 Tape the corners with masking tape.

2 It takes 12 sticks to make a cube. If you want to make it stronger, you'll need to turn squares into triangles, and that will take more sticks.

3 It takes 4 or 5 cubes to reach the ceiling. Test the strength of 1 cube by pressing down gently. If it twists down, it can't be strong enough to support another 4 or 5 cubes on top of it.

4 Add another stick where the dotted line is. Do the same thing on every side of the cube. Now press down again gently. The cube does not twist down. That's because a triangle is a very stable and strong shape. Make the rest of your cubes with triangles, and you can build a skyscraper as tall as your room - really.

Lay your tower on its side between two chairs and you've built a bridge! You've also made a terrific toy out of a section of the newspaper!

P.S. from Beakman: Chicago is the birthplace of the skyscraper. One of Chicago's skyscrapers is the John Hancock Center, which wears its triangles on the outside. Stable triangles is how it got to be 98 stories tall.

Dear Beakman,

What is money made out of? Can you make it?

Bryan Eccleston
Spencer,
Massachusetts

Dear Bryan,

The simple answer is that money is made out of metal, paper, ink, stone, even plastic. The complicated answer is that money is made *mostly out of promises.*

The promise is from the government that made the money. It says that a piece of paper is worth a dollar. We trust that the government will last long enough to keep that promise. (One thing that helps a government be long-lasting is an army.)

You cannot make the same money that the government makes. That's called counterfeiting (COWN-tur-fit-ing) and it's a crime.

You Can earn money by knowing something or having a skill that others value. Anything else - like tricking someone - is like stealing.

Beakman
Beakman Place

Math Skills Are Valuable

WHAT YOU NEED: 50 pennies or other coins - a friend
Optional: 50 pebbles, 50 sticks

WHAT TO DO: Ask your friend to play a little game with you. Explain that you both can take turns removing up to four pennies from the pile of coins. The person who has the last turn wins. You will always be able to win and the reason is knowledge of math.

Part of the trick is convincing your friend to take the first turn. After that, it's subtraction and division.

MORE STUFF TO DO: Remember the number 5. Make sure that your coins plus the number your friend takes always add up to be 5. If your pal takes 4, you take 1.

If you continue to subtract the number of coins your friend takes from the number 5, and use the answer as the number of coins you take, you'll always get to take the last turn - and win.

SO WHAT: This works because 5 divides evenly into 50, and the most pennies *You Can* take at once is only 4. So *You Can* control how many turns there are.

The problem with this kind of thing as a bet to make money is it's a trick - *rigged*. Which means it's like stealing. You can't trick people out of their money and be a whole, happy, healthy person. At least that's what I think. You decide. How do you feel about it?

A Closer Look at Quarters

75% copper
25% nickel

100% copper

75% copper
25% nickel

You Can see 3 layers on a quarter. The shiny, silvery-looking top and bottom are there just for looks - to look like real silver. Quarters made before 1964 were made out of silver - a valuable metal. Even though today's quarters look like silver, there is *no silver or gold at all* in any U.S. coin that is used for money.

P.S. from Jax: The copper/nickel sandwich that U.S. coins are made from is created with explosions! An explosive is spread on the outside of the nickel layers. When it goes off, it bonds them to the copper center.

Dear Jax,

Why does wax form in our ears?

**David & Marisa
Denver, Colorado**

Dear David & Marisa,

Why something happens is a very tough question. It's like all cosmic to talk about *why things happen.* The purpose of earwax in the universe I can't guess.

But I can easily tell you what its job is in your body. It's protection.

Every place your body opens up to the outside world is protected by something to trap the gook, gunk and schmutz that want to get inside our bodies and pollute them.

Jax Place
Jax Place

Ohhhh! Icckkkk! Gross!

WHAT YOU NEED: Earwax - newspaper - water - butter

WHAT TO DO: The next time your ears get cleaned, smear a bit of the gross stuff onto a white piece of newspaper. Do the same thing with a drop of water and a bit of butter on other pieces of newspaper. Let them dry for an hour or two and then look at them again. Any difference?

SO WHAT: Earwax is thickened skin oils. It will grease up the newspaper and won't evaporate like the water. It'll make a greasy *stain* on the newspaper, like the butter.

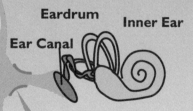

Eardrum   Inner Ear

Ear Canal

The tunnel that's open to the world from your ear has curved walls. It gets narrow in the middle. Earwax is a collection of skin oils that ooze out of the walls of this tunnel. It coats the narrow part of the tunnel. Dust and gunk get caught in it. In the microscopic photo of earwax *You Can* see that it has trapped dust, hair and gunk.

Ears, Oils and Safety

Your ear canal is a self-cleaning system. When left alone, the ear canal oozes out thick oils, which then catch junk and schmutz. That hardens the oils into waxy chunks that will just fall out on their own.

You should not stick a cotton swab into your ear. That would pack down the wax against the eardrum. It won't fall out, and you're in danger of hurting your eardrum—a very sensitive and delicate thing.

Famous dead artist and ear-safety poster boy, Vincent van Gogh.

P.S. from Beakman: Oil is oozing out of your body all over your skin. In fact, every hair is coated with oil as it grows up and out of your body. It's why shiny hair shines.

Dear Jax,

Why are there all these cracking sounds in my room at night?

**Tiffany Yoder
Cerro Gordo,
Illinois**

Dear Tiffany,

What you're hearing is not a dream - it's not something you're making up for yourself.

The sound does not come from under your bed. Creaky creepy monsters do not live there.

That sound is real. It comes from your house or apartment and the things inside it.

The sound happens when things change size. They change size when they change temperatures. Really!

Jax Place
Jax Place

Expansion and Contraction

EXPERIMENT #1

WHAT YOU NEED: Glass soda bottle - balloon - ice cubes - bowl

WHAT TO DO: Put the balloon over the top of the bottle and let it flop over. Put the bottle in the bowl and pour the ice cubes into the bowl all around the bottle. Watch the balloon and wait for a while - like, maybe 8 minutes. What happens?

WHAT IS GOING ON: The air in the bottle and in the balloon got cold. When it got cold, it got smaller. We call that contraction (cun-TRAC-shun). The air in the bottle contracted so much that the balloon was pulled inside the bottle.

DAY
(Warm)

NIGHT
(Cool)

If you put the bottle out in the sunshine, the air in the bottle will absorb heat energy and will get bigger. We call that expansion (x-PAN-shun). The air will expand so much that the balloon will inflate and stand up.

Warm things usually expand (get bigger). Cold things usually contract (get smaller).

P.S. from Beakman: All this popping, snapping and cracking happens in the morning, too. We don't hear it as well because we're up and busy and making our own noises in the morning.

So What

Things That Go Bump in the Night

In your experiment, air and the balloon contracted and expanded. Both are flexible, soft or stretchy. They don't make sounds when they change size.

Your house is built from things that are not stretchy, very soft or very flexible. When your house gets bigger or smaller, it will make popping and cracking sounds. This is also true for the furniture in your room.

When the sun goes down and things cool off, your house and the stuff inside it will contract - get smaller and make loud cracking or popping sounds.

Warm wires expand and sag.

Cold wires contract and tighten up.

Other Things to Look For

When builders make roads and bridges, they make sure to put in places for expansion and contraction. The black lines in a sidewalk are expansion joints.

Something as simple as the difference between daytime and nightime temperatures is enough to crack concrete, snap telephone wires, or even bend steel electrical towers if they are not built properly.

183

Dear Jax,

Can you really get to the other side of the rainbow?

Shelley Kovine
Tel Aviv, Israel

Dear Shelley,

Rainbows are very personal things. The rainbow you see is just yours. Your rainbow will always be in front of you. Ahead of you.

You Can be on the other side of another person's rainbow. But that won't be your rainbow and you won't be able to see it.

Rainbows happen only when things are lined up in a special way. To be on the other side of a rainbow wrecks that special line-up, and the rainbow does not form.

Jax Place
Jax Place

Man-Made Rainbows

WHAT YOU NEED: Sunny day - garden hose - friend

WHAT TO DO: Set the spray on the nozzle until you get a fine, fine mist of water. Turn around until you see a rainbow. Ask your friend to stand about 15 feet in front of you - on the other side of your rainbow.

Ask your friend to look back toward you and your rainbow. Does he or she see your rainbow? Trade places.

A rainbow is what happens when sunlight shines into water droplets. The white light is taken apart into its separate colors.

1
SUN

2 **3** **4**

5

1 - The Sun
2 - The person looking at the rainbow
3 - The rain (or hose spray)
4 - No. 2's personal rainbow
5 - The guy who's on the other side who's not going to see it.

Rainbows being out in front of you is also the reason why you can't get to the end of a rainbow that you can see. As you move closer to the rainbow, it seems to move farther away.

SO WHAT: You're going to find that the 1, 2, 3, 4 order is needed to get a rainbow. It will be a rainbow only you can see. Your friend is on the other side but isn't inside the 1 to 4 line-up and can't see anything special.

P.S. from Beakman: People want the other side of the rainbow to feel all magical. It won't unless you create that magic yourself. And you know You Can!

186

Dear Beakman,

What is the problem with the ozone layer? What is the ozone layer? What can I do about it?

Kelly Brewer
Aurora, Colorado

Dear Kelly,

Those are questions a lot of readers have. I get hundreds of letters asking about the ozone. Ozone is a word we see and hear a lot in the news. And the news can scare us.

I know that there is a lot of fear about the ozone. But *You Can* turn fear into something else. What you change fear into is up to you. But before *You Can* change fear, you have to understand what's going on. It's how you begin.

Beakman

Beakman Place

What Is Ozone?

The circle drawings below are the shape of an ozone molecule. Ozone is made up of oxygen atoms. The oxygen we breathe is made from 2 atoms. It's called O_2. Ozone is made from 3 atoms and is called O_3. Ozone isn't very stable. It can break apart and turn into O_2 easily. There is lots of it high above the Earth near the edge of outer space.

Ozone is the right size and shape to absorb energy from the Sun that can be dangerous. The ozone forms a layer that absorbs some of the Sun's energy. That layer protects us.

The dangerous sunlight is called UV, which is short for ultraviolet. Some of this light shines on us every day. The big fear is that more of it might hurt us. UV light can change a part of our skin cells. It can make them duplicate themselves like crazy, like a copying machine gone nuts. That's all skin cancer is - uncontrolled copying of skin cells.

The fear of more sickness is what we have to change into something else. That's a big job, and we all need help with it. Big jobs are a lot easier when we work together. This problem is something *You Can* bring to your class at school and to your friends and family.

What Is the Problem?

To better understand the problem see the diagram on page 188. It shows how freon and other related chemicals drift up miles above the Earth to the part of our air called the stratosphere (STRAT-us-fear). That's where ozone is. When high energy sunlight (**1**) hits a freon molecule, it breaks up and releases a chlorine atom (**2**). The chlorine atom then bangs into an ozone molecule (**3**). That turns the ozone into regular oxygen (**4**). Regular oxygen (O_2) isn't the right size and shape to absorb the kind of sunlight that can be dangerous.

How Did All This Start?

A long time ago, refrigerators used a poisonous gas to move heat. Moving heat is how all refrigerators still work. The gas was ammonia gas, and it made refrigeration dangerous. Chemists worked very hard to invent a new gas that behaved like ammonia but wasn't poison. They invented freon (FREE-on), which is inert. Inert means it won't mix with anything else at all. It seemed perfect. People got to have refrigerators, and that was very good. But in the 1970s, scientists found out that if you add solar energy to a freon molecule it will split up. By then the gas was used in spray cans and to puff up plastic foam. People cut down on the use of freon. But they didn't stop using it. That's a problem.

SO WHAT: If you are concerned about the ozone layer, talk about it. Keep talking till someone listens. Someone will.

One of the things *You Can* change fear into is action. Use less plastic foam. Maybe get your class to write letters to our political leaders. Tell them how you feel. Or come up with something else on your own. You decide.

189

Dear Jax,

Why are photos in the newspaper all made of little dots?

**Justin Camaratto
Huntington,
California**

Dear Justin,

Pictures are kind of a problem in printing. Photos are not just black. There are many shades of gray in most black-and-white pictures.

The problem is that newspapers are printed with black ink - one color of black.

Even if the paper has color printing, it still has only one shade of black and no shades of gray at all.

So how do you print grays without different gray inks? The answer is those little dots you asked about. They are called a halftone screen.

Jax Place

Jax Place

See the Dots

WHAT YOU NEED: Clear tape - water - bobby pin

WHAT TO DO: Cover this photograph with the tape. Press it down tight and make sure it's completely covered.

Dip the folded end of the bobby pin into the water and touch it to Andy's eye - right in the middle of the picture. Leave just one drop of water. Look closely into the water drop. It becomes a magnifier.

WHAT IS GOING ON: The picture seems to have lots of grays in it, like Andy's hair and his face. But really, it's all made of little dots of pure black. Our minds can't read the dots as separate things because the dots are too small. Our brains add together the black dots and

P.S. from Beakman: Andy's last name is Warhol. He was an artist who loved printing and mass production.

Another Look at Dots

WHAT TO DO:
Look at this picture really close up.

Now stand it up on a table and move back till it makes sense.

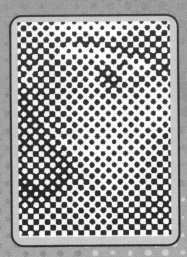

WHAT IS GOING ON: This is a close-up of the dots that make up Andy's left eye - the one in the center of the other picture. Up close, it doesn't look like much of anything. When we get far away, our minds start putting the dots together as shades of gray, and we can see an eye and his glasses.

Little Dots

The first circle is white. The last circle is black. And there are lots of shades of gray in between. The thing is, there aren't gray inks - just black. Look closely and you'll see the dots that fake the shades of gray.

When the dots are used like this, they're called a halftone screen. It's called 65 l.p.i. That means there are 65 lines per inch - or 65 dots per inch. Magazines print with smaller dots that are harder to see - at 133 l.p.i. or even smaller dots at 150 l.p.i.

Dear Beakman,

How do cellular phones work? What are the cells?

**Nick Sorum
Wrangell,
Arkansas**

Dear Nick,

Cells are about sharing. Before cellular technology, 1 big transmitter could use 200 radio channels to send phone calls to an entire city. Now, cellular phones use lots of low-powered transmitters inside little areas we call cells. The different cells can share the limited number of radio channels.

Computers keep track of which cell the little phones are in and send calls only to the antenna in that cell. If you had only 200 radio channels available and 250 cells, you'd be able to have 50,000 phone calls happening at the same time—spread out over all the cells. That's big-time sharing.

Beakman
Beakman Place

193

You're Breaking Up

Cute little blue Roadster A is leaving cell B and is traveling into cell C. The cellular phone in Roadster A has its own ID number that it transmits whenever it's on. That helps computers in the cellular telephone company building (D) keep track of which cell the phone is in.

The conversation is broadcast on FM radio waves from Roadster A to cellular antenna C. It then goes on land lines to the cellular phone company (red dotted lines) and on more land lines to the regular phone company (E) and then on to your house (F).

Conversations can get interrupted when Roadster A moves from cell B to cell C. Computers keep track of where the car is and have to switch the call from one antenna to the next. Lots of times that does not go very smoothly.

194

So What's with the Bee?

When circles are squeezed into each other, the shape they always make is a hexagon. A hexagon is the shape with the least circumference (the line around the outside) and the maximum area inside that will *tile*.

When a shape tiles, it fits against other shapes just like itself in a pattern with no empty space left in between.

That makes it the perfect shape for storing things (like the most honey with the least wax) or for getting squeezed together into phone cells.

P.S. from Jax: Bees like hexagons because they use the least wax to store the most honey. *You Can* also see circles squeezed together into hexagons in the kitchen sink. Bubbles and suds tile into little hexagons!

Dear Beakman,

I like to clean. How does my vacuum suck up dirt?

Giovanni Lizama Hyattsville, Maryland

Dear Giovanni,

"Suck" is a confusing idea. It's a lot like darkness and cold. The business end of cold is really more or less heat. There is no such thing as cold. The business end of darkness is more or less light. Darkness is not a thing you can make.

Sucking is like that, too. The business end of sucking is something else *pushing* harder - like in a shoving match.

The motor and fan inside your vacuum cleaner lower the air pressure inside it. That means the air pressure outside is higher - and pushing harder - into the vacuum cleaner. It will push dust and schmutz with it. They get caught in a filter.

Beakman

Beakman Place

Sucking Up or Pushing In?

EXPERIMENT #1

WHAT YOU NEED: Glass of soda or water - straw - a new perspective

WHAT TO DO: Take a drink with your straw. Do it again and pay attention to what's happening. Use this explanation to get a new perspective (new angle) on how it works: We live at the bottom of an ocean of air. It's pushing down on us all the time. That pushing is why your straw works!

When you use a straw, you're really setting up a shoving match. In a shoving match, whoever pushes the hardest wins.

When you lower the air pressure in your mouth, the higher air pressure on top of the soda (1) will now push down harder. The only place the soda can go is up the straw (2) and into your mouth (3).

A vacuum cleaner works the same way. It's higher air pressure outside the machine that pushes air into it. As the air pushes in, it pushes gunk with it.

197

A Look Inside

All vacuum cleaners work the same way. The only differences are details like whether or not it has a rotating brush or different attachments. The motor (1) turns a fan that lowers the air pressure between the fan and the filter bag (2). That means the air pressure outside the vacuum cleaner (3) is higher and it will rush in, pushing in little bits of crud. The crud gets caught in the filter bag.

Everything that's inside your vacuum cleaner got there because it was pushed inside. None of it was sucked in there, because nothing can get sucked. Despite what Bart Simpson says, *nothing sucks*. It either gets pushed or it pushes. Period.

P.S. from Jax: Think of another word - like vacuum - that has 2 U's in a row!

198

Dear Jax,

How do you make paper?

**Marisa Van Buskirk
Berkeley Heights,
New Jersey**

Dear Marisa,

Paper is made from cellulose (SELL-u-los), which is in plant fibers. The cellulose is made by grinding up trees and dumping the pulp in acid. But recycling uses cellulose over and over again.

Recycled paper can be made with less electricity, with less water, with a lot less pollution, and it saves trees from being cut down.

Jax Place

Jax Place

Recycled Paper Procedure

Follow this step by step.

First, some information:

⚠ Making recycled paper is messy. It is also a lot of fun. Someone will have to use a food processor and an electric iron. Both can be dangerous. So make sure that you get help on this project because it is a big one. It is best to do this with some friends and family. That way you can spread the mess and the fun around.

WHAT YOU NEED: Two full newspaper pages torn into 2-inch squares - food processor - 2 tablespoons white glue - 2 or 3 cups water - sink with 4 inches water - old panty hose - coat hangers - electric iron
OPTIONAL: *insect screen - strainer - food coloring - dryer lint*

Step 1

Undo the coat hanger and use the wire to make a flat square about 6 by 6 inches big. Stretch one leg of the panty hose over it. Take your time; it could snag. If you put tape on the ends of the wire, it will snag less. Make sure it is *tight and flat*. Tie knots in the hose. Use the other leg for another piece of paper. You will need one frame for every piece of paper you make. You might want to make more than one or two.

Make your frame like this.

P.S. from Beakman: Don't be fooled. When a box or a bag says that it is 100% recyclable that means that you can recycle it. It does not mean that it is made out of recycled paper.

Step 2

Put a handful of the paper and some water into the food processor. Close the food processor and turn it on high. Keep adding paper and water until you have a big gray blob. You may have to add a little more water to keep things moving smoothly. Keep the food processor on until all the paper has *disappeared*. Then leave it on for 2 whole minutes. Put the glue in the sink water and add all of the paper pulp you just made. Mix it really well. Use your hands.

Mix up the sink water again and then scoop the frame to the bottom of the sink. Lift it real slow. Count to 20 slowly while you are lifting. Let the water drain out for about a minute. Mix up the sink every time you make a new piece.

Step 3

The ink in the newspaper makes the paper pulp look like a blob of gross gray gunk.

Try other things like the screen or a strainer. Try adding *lots* of food coloring, or lint, or leaves, to the food processor.

Now you have to hang the frames on a clothesline or put them out in the sun. Wait until they are completely dry with *no dampness at all*. *You Can* then gently peel off the paper. Have a grown-up use the iron - set on the hottest setting - to steam out your paper. *You Can* keep making paper until the pulp is all strained out of the sink.

See how strong your paper is. Trim it with scissors. Write on it. It is strong.

Dear Jax,

Why do balloons pop and why do they make a loud bang?

Joseph Huff
Pensacola, Florida

Dear Joseph,

How a thing happens or doesn't happen is usually science.

Why it happens or doesn't happen is usually called philosophy (fil-OS-o-fee).

For right now, let's stick with *how* a balloon does what it does. That's a way easier question.

Here are 2 big words: tensile cohesion (TEN-sill co-HE-shun). They mean *stretchy strength*. Balloons break when they get expanded beyond the limits of their tensile cohesion - beyond the limits of their stretchy strength.

Jax Place
Jax Place

Make a Joyful Noise

WHAT YOU NEED: Paper bag

WHAT TO DO: Blow up the bag and pop it. Think about it as you do it.

SO WHAT: When you pop a bag, you're squeezing the air inside the bag, forcing it into a smaller size. The air will push back out until it's the same size as it was. The pushing back is the *bang*.

SO WHAT: When something small gets big really quickly, we call it an explosion. The loud bang is air exploding back to the size it was before you squeezed it.

Balloons squeeze air, too.

EXPERIMENT #2

WHAT YOU NEED: Balloon - bamboo skewer

WHAT TO DO: Blow up the balloon and tie its end with a knot. Find the spot at the top of the balloon that is darker in color. Gently twist the skewer into the very top and out near the knot at the bottom. If you're careful, the balloon will not pop.

SO WHAT: The balloon is made from latex, a substance that's built like long stretchy springs. When these springs get stretched too long, they snap and the balloon pops.

Relaxed

Stretched

The top and bottom of the balloon are like springs that are relaxed and are not pulling away. Everywhere else on the balloon, these springs are stretched tight near the limit of their strength - near the limits of their tensile cohesion.

P.S. from Beakman: The word *balloon* is from an old Germanic word *balla* that means ball. Another kind of balloon is the one you see in the funnies. A balloon is the thing a comic strip character's words are inside of.

Dear Beakman,

How do you make paint?

**Anne Gregory
Sacramento,
California**

Dear Anne,

Paints are all just about the same. They all have pigment - which is the color - and a vehicle - the liquid in which the color is carried. Paint started as a way to decorate cave walls with pictures. Now paint is also a protection. The right kind of vehicle in the paint can keep out weather and water. If you make some paint, keep in mind that there will always be someone around to tell you how to use it. These people are called critics (CRIT-icks), and they'd rather tell you how to paint than paint themselves.

Beakman Place

EXPERIMENT #1

You Can Make Some Paint

WHAT YOU NEED: A brick - hammer - old cooking pan - eggs - water - ⚠ safety glasses or sunglasses

WHAT TO DO: Put on the glasses. They'll protect your eyes. Use the hammer to knock off a chunk of the brick's corner. Use a red brick. Smash up the chunk of brick into tiny pieces and put them in the pot. (This isn't very easy. But they say that artists have to suffer. Maybe this is what that means.) Add a little spoonful of water. Now use the handle of the hammer to pound the brick bits till you get a paste. If you're clever, you can talk someone into helping you because this will take time.

MORE STUFF TO DO: For every 2 tablespoons of paste you have, you'll need 1 egg yolk. Ask a grown-up to show you how to separate an egg. Mix up the yolk with a fork till it looks lemony. Now add the paste and stir it up really well. You just made paint. The brick dust is colored red by a chemical called iron oxide (rust). It's the pigment. The egg yolks are the vehicle.

Another Kind of Paint You Can Make

WHAT YOU NEED: Colored chalk - white glue - the hammer and pot and glasses from Experiment #1

WHAT TO DO: Instead of pounding on bricks for a long time, try grinding up and pounding on chalk. It's a lot easier. You'll be surprised at the small amount of powder you'll get. There's a lot of air in chalk.

Grind your chalk dust with a little water just like in the first experiment. For every two sticks of chalk, use 1 tablespoon of white glue. Mix it all up real well.

Try mixing different colored chalks. One red stick of chalk and another that's yellow should give you orange paint. Experiment on your own with vehicles and pigments. Soft rocks are good for some colors. The soot from inside a fireplace will give you black. An important part of art is experimenting.

The most expensive paint there is is made from a gemstone. Real ultramarine blue paint is used by artists, but not very often because it costs a lot. It's made by grinding up the gem lapis lazuli - a beautiful blue gem. Most of the ultramarine blue paint sold is imitation.

207

Dear Beakman,

Where does gravity come from? What is the short answer?

Rebecca Bergaust Marietta, Georgia

Dear Beakman,

How does the Moon control the tides?

Jasmine Senaveratna Baltimore, Maryland

Dear Rebecca and Jasmine,

You guys should meet. You're both asking the same question.

The short answer on gravity is that it's a force of nature. Gravity is an *attraction* between any 2 objects. Gravity is not pushing you down to the Earth. You are pulled to it, and the Earth is pulled to you. You're 1 object. The Earth is the second object. You need at least 2 objects.

Gravity between the Moon and the oceans and - to a lesser extent - between the Sun and the oceans power the oceans' tides.

Beakman

Beakman Place

You Really Move Me!

The oceans pull toward the Moon and the Moon pulls toward the oceans. Ditto for the Sun. Water moves easily. It's a fluid. That means we can see high and low tide at seaside.

In the drawing on the next page, the Sun is directly opposite the Moon. That makes for a full Moon and a very high tide. (The tide in the drawing is exaggerated so *You Can* see it.)

WHAT YOU NEED: Water faucet - comb - dry day

WHAT TO DO: Comb your hair in the same direction for 40 or 50 strokes. Futz with the water faucet until you get a steady, skinny stream.

Bring the comb down near the stream of water. Do not touch the stream with the comb. Just be near it. Pull the comb back. What happens?

WHAT IS GOING ON: Your comb carried a charge of static electricity. It is another force of nature. It is *not* gravity.

But, it can attract water and pull it.

On a much, much bigger scale, gravity between the Moon and the oceans is pulling the water outward, raising the tides.

MOON   HIGH TIDE   EARTH   ATTRACTION   SUN

ATTRACTION

LOW TIDE

P.S. from Jax: Gravity pulls on the solid parts of the Earth, too. The stresses that it causes are sometimes blamed for causing earthquakes.

210

Dear Beakman,

Where does gravity come from? What is the short answer?

Rebecca Bergaust
Marietta, Georgia

Dear Beakman,

How does the Moon control the tides?

Jasmine Senaveratna
Baltimore, Maryland

Dear Rebecca
and Jasmine,

First we talked about how gravity is an attraction between any 2 objects. We also talked about how gravity between the Moon and the oceans pulls the water and makes a high tide.

Now we want you to try a gravity experiment first done by Galileo in 1620.

Galileo was a little like the singer Madonna. Both get along with just a first name and both seem to upset a lot of people with the stuff they think.

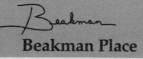

Beakman Place

Is Heavier Faster?

WHAT YOU NEED: Apple - piece of paper - chair

WHAT TO DO: Get up on the chair. Hold the apple in one hand and the paper in the other. Lift them up high and let them go. Do not toss or push or throw. Just let go.

MORE STUFF: Wad the paper up into as tight a ball as *You Can*. When you repeat the experiment, it will be way different. Check the upside-down line to see how that worked.

Back in the 1500s everyone thought that the bigger something was, the faster it would fall. The authorities didn't like people questioning things like this. They wanted to control every-thing. But Galileo questioned it anyway and his thinking got him in trouble.

He thought that if 2 bricks fell side by side at the same speed, it doesn't make any sense for them to double their speed just because they were cemented together.

The single bricks were small and would fall at the same speed. But the cemented bricks were bigger, and if bigger things fall faster, then they would have to fall faster. But what was it about sticking them together that could change their speed? The whole bigger-falls-faster idea was falling apart and didn't make much sense.

When Galileo proved he was right with today's experiment, he got fired from his job teaching at a university. His thinking was just too dangerous. He questioned authority.

Later Galileo committed a much bigger thought-crime. He said that the Earth was not the center of the universe. He was imprisoned even though he was right.

Which Falls Faster?

P.S. from Jax: The flat piece of paper fell slowly because of air resistance - air pushing against it. When you wadded it up, the paper fell at the same speed as the apple.

Dear Beakman,

How can I make flowers into perfume?

**Troy Manard
Olathe, Kansas**

Dear Troy,

If you want to make perfume, get ready to pick lots and lots of flowers. It takes more than a ton of rose petals to get enough rose oil to fill a coffee cup.

Perfume is made out of plant oils, oils from animals and lots of synthetics (sin-THET-icks) - chemicals made in laboratories that copy chemicals in nature.

Real perfume is blended oils only, and is very strong. Cologne is perfume that has been mixed with alcohol and water to make it weaker. We say the perfume is diluted (di-LUT-ed) into cologne.

Beakman

Beakman Place

What Is a Rose Like Anyway?

EXPERIMENT #1

WHAT YOU NEED: Scissors - tack - pencil - trip to the photocopier

WHAT TO DO: Photocopy the pink circle below at the same size, cut it out, and use the tack to attach the center to the eraser of a pencil. When you spin it counterclockwise, you get the answer to the question above.

It's a poem by the famous dead poet Gertrude Stein. The poem goes on and on because there's no other answer to the question.

A rose is A rose is A rose is A rose is

A rose is A rose is

Enfleurage (en-flur-AHJ) is how perfumers get oils from flower petals. The petals are spread over glass plates that have been covered with fat. The glass plates are pressed together and the flower oils mix with the fat. The fat is then scraped off and mixed with alcohol. The alcohol mixes with the flower oils. Next, the alcohol containing the flower oils is separated from the fats. Finally, the alcohol is removed by a process called distillation. That leaves a teeny drop of pure essential oil.

Enfleurage is one reason why whales were hunted to near-extinction. Until recently, the fat that was used came from dead whales.

Up Close and Personal

This is a rose petal photographed through an electron microscope. These little bumps are all filled with a tiny droplet of rose oil.

When you brush your finger across most flower petals, they feel soft and velvety.

These little bumps are what you're really dragging your finger across.

Try it the next time you see a flower.

Electron micrograph: Wilfred Bentham

P.S. from Jax: Many drugstores sell essential oils. *You Can* use them to create a perfume. Use a dropper to mix different fragrances together until you get one you like. Perhaps you'll name it *Manard No.5*.

Dear Tiffany,

The stuff that goes down the drain is 99 percent pure water and only 1 percent solid waste. That means we're making an awful lot of pure water dirty - just to move a tiny bit of junk we want to get rid of.

How much? Well, the city of Los Angeles dirties 440,000,000 gallons *every day*. Feature that on a planetary scale. Yow! It's enough to scare you!

All the water we have on Earth is all we'll ever get. Sewage is water we've borrowed from the planet. We have to clean it before giving it back. If we don't, something is seriously wrong.

Beakman

Beakman Place

Make Some Sewage

WHAT YOU NEED: Used coffee grounds - oil - dinner leftovers - blender or food processor - jar with lid - help and permission from an adult

WHAT TO DO: Chop up half your leftovers into bits. ⚠ *If you're not allowed to use a knife, ask an adult in your family to do this for you.* Purée the rest in the blender with a little oil.

This will be gross. Use a big spoon to add $1/4$ cup of chopped stuff and $1/4$ cup of puréed stuff to the jar. Then add $1/2$ cup of used coffee grounds and fill with water.

SO WHAT: After you shake this up, let it sit *very still* for 2 hours. Look at it now. It's separated into layers: light oils on top, then heavier fats. Next comes dirty water and then several layers of heavy solids at the bottom.

Cleaning the water means we have to (1) skim off the oils and fat, (2) let the solids settle so we can separate them and (3) filter the water until it's clear and clean. Only then should we give back the water we've borrowed. Cleaned water is put back into rivers, lakes and the oceans.

P.S. from Jax: The shapes above are water molecules - 2 hydrogen atoms and 1 oxygen atom. That why it's called H_2O.

Clean Some Sewage

EXPERIMENT #2

WHAT YOU NEED: Coffee filter - funnel or coffee cone - sewage from Experiment #1 - turkey baster - clean sand - jar
Optional: charcoal bits from aquarium filter

WHAT TO DO: Put the coffee filter into the funnel or cone. If you have the charcoal, add a tablespoon. Fill the filter paper all the way with clean sand. Set it in a new jar.

Use the baster to skim the oil and fats from your sewage jar. This is waste.

Now use the baster to suck up just the dirty water layer from the jar. Add this to your funnel of sand and let it drip through. It'll be a lot cleaner.

SO WHAT: You just did what most sewage treatment plants do to millions of gallons of water every day. And they filter it over and over till it's clean.

A terrific class project is to invite people from your local sewer district to visit your school. They'll bring samples of real sewage if you ask.

You Can make a fantastic funnel by cutting the bottom off a plastic soda bottle.

219

Dear Beakman,

How did they invent Scotch™ tape?

Antoinette Freeman
Calistoga, California

Dear Antoinette,

Scotch™ tape has something in common with recording tape and those little yellow sticky pieces of paper called Post-It Notes™.

They are all based on sandpaper! Really. The people who made sandpaper learned best how to put really fine layers of different stuff together.

Minnesota Mining and Manufacturing, or 3M, learned how to do fine layering when it improved the sandpaper it made. It gave 3M a head start on inventing masking tape, which was later turned into Scotch™ tape.

Beakman
Beakman Place

Drew Brews New Glue!

Famous Dead Guy In Science & Marketing

Richard Drew
1899–1980

3M sold lots of its sandpaper to car factories. Then, in 1923, cars with 2 colors got to be way popular. They were called *two-toned*. Autoworkers asked the 3M salespeople if they knew of something that would hold newspaper onto the cars so they could spray-paint a second color.

Mr. Drew worked at 3M and started experimenting with rubber cements, finely layered onto strips of paper. He called it masking tape.

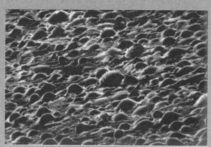

Electron micrograph: Wilfred Bentham

This shows you how finely the glue has to be layered. This is a microscopic view of the sticky strip of a Post-It Note™. It's pretty much tape with a special glue that can *un*-stick.

Release Agent
Plastic Film
Primer
Adhesive

Scotch™ tape has 4 fine layers.

The Name That Stuck

Unfortunately, sometimes people use the name of a whole nationality as an insult to *dis* people. Name-calling is not a good thing. But "Scotch" used to mean cheap or stingy.

Autoworkers didn't like the first tape Mr. Drew invented. They wanted more adhesive on the tape so that it wouldn't fall off. They called it Scotch tape. They meant the tape was *cheap*, and the people who made it were *stingy* with the glue.

The 3M company didn't like that and made much stickier tape that worked really well. But the nickname *Scotch tape* stuck to the product. "Scotch" could also mean *thrifty*, so 3M made the word its trademark for its products.

P.S. from Jax: All the little ™ marks on this section show you that the 3M company actually owns the word "Scotch" as a brand name. Other things, like the adult drink, can still be called Scotch. But not any other kind of tape product.

Dear Beakman,

How do CD players work?

**Tristan Nenna
South Bend,
Indiana**

Dear Tristan,

The best way to understand how a CD player works is to make a *Mind Movie*. That's what I call making up a complicated vision with the power of your imagination.

To make a *Mind Movie*, get a friend or member of your family. Close your eyes and get all peaceful-like while your helper reads out loud from this book.

Imagine the things you're being told.

Beakman

Beakman Place

CD Player:
The Mind Movie

Read this out loud in an even-toned voice. Don't rush this.
Give the listener lots of time to use her or his imagination.

Imagine you're in a long, long hallway. It's so long you can't see the beginning in front of you or the end behind you. The hallway is miles and miles long. You look up. Somehow, someone has put bathtubs upside down on the ceiling. In between the bathtubs are mirrors. As far as you can see up and down the ceiling of the hallway are bathtubs and mirrors. For miles of ceiling there are bathtubs and mirrors, upside down on the ceiling. Then, everything gets dark!

You have a flashlight in one hand. You turn on the light, point it up to the ceiling and start running. Every time the light shines up and hits a mirror, the light bounces right back down at you. But when the light goes into a tub, it scatters and gets lost and you're left in the dark.

Now imagine that you can take notes while you're running. Every time the light bounces back down, you write a 1. When the light gets lost, you write a zero. After running for miles and miles, you'd have a whole sheet of paper filled with 1's and 0's. And those numbers are what a CD player uses to play back music and data. Now open your eyes and come back.

A real CD player doesn't use a flashlight. It uses a laser. And your weird ceiling is really a shiny disk covered with pits. If a CD didn't spin and were a hallway - like in your Mind Movie - it would be more than 4 miles long.

CDs play upside down, with the laser pointing up. The beginning of the disk is the center of the disk - the opposite of how a phonograph record works. (A phonograph record is what they used in olden times to listen to bands with names like *Strawberry Alarm Clock*.)

A CD player plays a sound that is based on numbers. It sees a new number 41,000 times a second!

P.S. from Jax: The width of a CD's track is so narrow you could lay 40 of them side by side under 1 human hair!

Dear Jax,

What is the strongest part of your body?

Steve Bittner
Winnipeg,
Ontario

Dear Steve,

There are many ways to be strong: strong of body, strong in spirit, strong of mind. Your mind can be so strong that *You Can* do something no one else can do using muscular strength - tear a phone book in half.

Okay, make sure that it's an *old* one, about 1 inch thick, that no one wants. And be patient, which is another kind of strength.

Don't give up till you've learned this technique (tec-NEEK).

Jax Place

More than One Way to Be Strong

WHAT YOU NEED: Old phone book - a friend who didn't read this

WHAT TO DO: Ask your friends if they have the strength to rip a phone book in 2. Explain that this is not a trick. We're talking really rip it, without precutting or any other gimmick.

Your friends won't think of intelligence. They'll think of muscular strength. And no one has enough of that strength to tear the book in half. You have to use your head.

The book will make a peak like in the big drawing.

top

Peel back the covers. Hold the book like this. Your thumbs should be together and your fingers *as far apart as possible.* Now squeeze the book and slide your fingers together *toward the middle.*

P.S. from Beakman: If you can't use a phone book, use a Sears catalog. The Sears people decided to stop selling stuff from that big book, which makes it perfect for ripping up.

Get a Grip

With your index fingers pushed toward each other, squeeze the book with your thumbs and fingers. Look at the red arrows. Bend the book back the way the arrows are pointing.

If the pages are in that special peak shape, the book will tear in half. The peak shape makes it possible for all your effort to be focused on 1 page at a time - rapidly tearing 1 after another.

You'll blow everyone's mind!

Thumb

Thumb

Dear Beakman,

How does the quartz crystal in a watch work?

**Billy Dellvow
Bath, Michigan**

Dear Billy,

I love this question because *You Can* have such a great time getting the answer.

A quartz watch is the opposite of a Lifesaver™ sparking in your mouth! Isn't that cool?

You'll have to go into the closet for this - but just until you see the light.

Beakman
Beakman Place

Sparks in the Dark

WHAT YOU NEED: Mirror - roll of *Cryst-O-Mint* flavor Lifesaver™ candy - closet - towel

WHAT TO DO: Go into the closet and stuff the towel under the door so no light at all gets in. Look around for several minutes to adjust your eyes to the darkness. Pop one of the Lifesavers into your mouth. Look into the mirror and crunch down. You'll see your mouth light up with a white flash. Cool, huh?

P.S. from Jax: We know people all over the world read *You Can*. So, you might be in a country that doesn't sell Lifesavers™ candy. Try others. Look for a clear or white mint that is almost all sugar crystals. Experiment with several until you find one that works for you!

WHAT IS GOING ON: You just created *piezo electricity* (pee-AY-zo). Here's what it is: If you put *physical energy* into some crystals, they change it into electrical energy. The reverse is true, too. If you put *electrical energy* into these crystals, you get physical energy back out. That's how a quartz crystal watch works. A battery puts electrical energy into the quartz crystal, which vibrates at controlled speeds - such as 30,000 times a second. A computer chip then counts the vibrations to figure out the time. 30,000 vibrations equals 1 second.

Dear Beakman,

Why does the wind blow?

Jenny Gillis
Kaukauna,
Wisconsin

Dear Jenny,

Nature likes things balanced. That goes for heat, too. It tries to balance temperatures. The wind blows because the Earth is not heated evenly by the Sun. The air moves up and down because of heat and cold. When that happens, more air rushes in to take its place. That is wind. Because the Earth is round and because it spins, the Sun's heat will never be even. So the wind will keep on blowing.

Beakman
Beakman Place

Uneven Heating

WHAT YOU NEED: Flashlight - dark room

WHAT TO DO: Hold the light straight toward the wall and turn it on. Now tilt the light so that it's shining on the wall near the ceiling. Notice how the light spreads out.

WHAT IS GOING ON: You just made a model of the Earth and Sun. Because the world is ball-shaped - or spherical (SFIR-i-kel) - the light spreads out at the North and South Poles. It's stronger at the middle, which is called the equator. This is why it's hot at the equator and cold at the North and South Poles.

Up here the light is spread out and is weaker.

At the equator the light and heat are focused tightly and are stronger.

Warm Things Go Up, Cold Things Go Down

WHAT YOU NEED: Candle - a grown-up - food coloring - water - ice cube tray

WHAT TO DO: Fill the ice cube tray with water and add 4 drops of red or green coloring to two cubes. When they're frozen solid, gently place 1 cube into a clear glass of water. Let the water get calm first. Look quickly and closely. The second cube is a spare. It helps to have a light on behind the glass. ⚠ Have the grown-up light the candle. You blow it out. Watch where the smoke goes.

WHAT IS GOING ON: The smoke rose up into the air because it's warmer than the rest of the air. As it rose, it also cooled. When the temperatures were balanced, the smoke stopped going up and just spread out.

The colored ice cube gave off swirls of color like the drawing, and they sank to the bottom of the glass. The colored water was colder than the clear water, so it flowed down. Hot and cold air behave the same - hot air goes up, cold air goes down.

So What:
You Don't Need a Weatherman to Know Which Way the Wind Blows*

Air rising and falling is much bigger and more powerful than your experiment, and it's what drives all the wind. Hot air at the equator lifts up from the ground like your smoke. When it does, something has to take the place of the air that just went up. Cold air from the North and South Poles is sucked down toward the equator. This causes enormous winds. It all has to do with uneven heating by the Sun. That means that all wind and power from wind mills started with the energy in the Sun.

*This is a line from a song written a long time ago by a man named Bob Dylan. What it means is sometimes we can figure things out for ourselves - that we don't need experts as often as we think we do.

Dear Beakman,

What is leap year? Why does it happen?

Fred Mortensen
Chicago, Illinois

Dear Fred,

We need leap day to keep whole days in our calendar.

Humans keep time by watching how long the planets take to move. But these movements don't always match up with each other. We say they are not synchronized (SINK-ron-eyezd).

The Earth spins around once every 24 hours. That's one day. A year has nothing to do with how many times the Earth spins.

One year lasts as long as the Earth takes to travel all the way around the Sun. The Earth takes $365\frac{1}{4}$ days to travel around the Sun.

Beakman
Beakman Place

Leap Year: The Mind Movie

WHAT YOU NEED: An active imagination - a helper to read this to you

WHAT TO DO: Close your eyes and get all peaceful. Ask your helper to read this out loud in a smooth, steady voice.

Imagine that you're inside of a bicycle shop. There are bicycles all over the place - standing in rows, hanging from the ceiling. There is a check-out counter with a piggy bank on top. You are there, too. You are the bicycle mechanic.

Your job is to spin the bicycle pedals and make sure the gears work right.

You push the pedals around once in a circle. But at the back of the bike, things get radical. The little gear spins and spins around hundreds of times. For every one spin of the front pedals, there are 365 spins of the rear wheel.

That is how most people think time works: that there is a link between 365 days and 1 year.

But you examine the gears more closely and - big surprise - there is *no chain*. There's nothing that locks them together. The wheels and the pedals could move at any speed they wanted. It's an extreme bike. Open your eyes and come back from the bike shop.

The pedals are like one year. Every time they go around, the Earth has spun about 365 times. But not *exactly* 365 times. The spin of the Earth is not linked to how long it takes for the Earth to go around the Sun. There is no bicycle chain.

The gears are not connected. A year does not divide evenly into a set number of exact days. It doesn't have to. A year takes 365 days, 5 hours, 48 minutes and 6 seconds - about 365¼ days.

Problem: The calendar has no quarter-days!

Solution: Save quarter-days in the piggy bank. Every four years you'll have one whole complete day. *You Can* take it out of the bank and add it to the calendar. That's what happens on February 29. It's a whole day we've saved up in pieces.

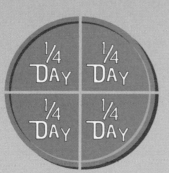

P.S. from Jax: Astronomers were the first timekeepers. Today astronomers do the same thing. When the extra seconds add up, they'll add them to our clocks - usually at midnight on Leap Day.

Dear Beakman,

Down at the mall there are lots of people with their eyes crossed, looking at 3-D posters. How do they work?
Robert Goldstone
Bloomington, Indiana

Dear Robert,

We recognize things like form, color and distance.

In the 1960s a psychologist named Bela Julesz made 3-D pictures with random dots - visual noise - to see if people could perceive distance without any clues from form or color. His 3-D dot pictures work because humans get used to patterns: repetitive, regular, predictable, repetitive. The pictures give us a regular pattern that is upset slightly.

Our minds move the upset pattern forward or backward to make it seem like it fits into the pattern again. That's what reveals the hidden images. It also feels very trippy and spacey.

Beakman
Beakman Place

Seeing Things

WHAT YOU NEED: Just your sweet self

WHAT TO DO: Look at the flies on the wall. Notice the 4 dots above the flies. Cross your eyes *slightly,* until you see 5 dots. Let your attention drift back down to the flies. They'll be floating!

Next, put the page right up to your nose. Focus your eyes as though you were looking across the room. Slowly take the page away from your face. If you start focusing on the page, *start over again.* Eventually, you'll see the flies float again. Only this time the little flies will be closest to you and the big ones will be farthest away. The distances will be reversed.

WHAT IS GOING ON: Both methods work because each of your eyes sees its own separate part of the fly pattern. Each part of the fly pattern is different, so your brain works to put them together by adding the sense of depth. The second method is called *averted view* and is how most of the 3-D posters work. If you cross your eyes at the posters, you'll reverse the distances and lose the hidden image. You'll see holes where you should be seeing things like whales or dolphins. Practice *averted view* on this simple version before your next trip to the mall. *And give yourself time!*

P.S. from Jax: Sometimes when we get spaced out (meditative), we can seem to see depth in things like carpeting, tree bark, sidewalk sparkles, acoustical ceiling tile or certain wallpapers. It's the same effect without a trip to the mall.

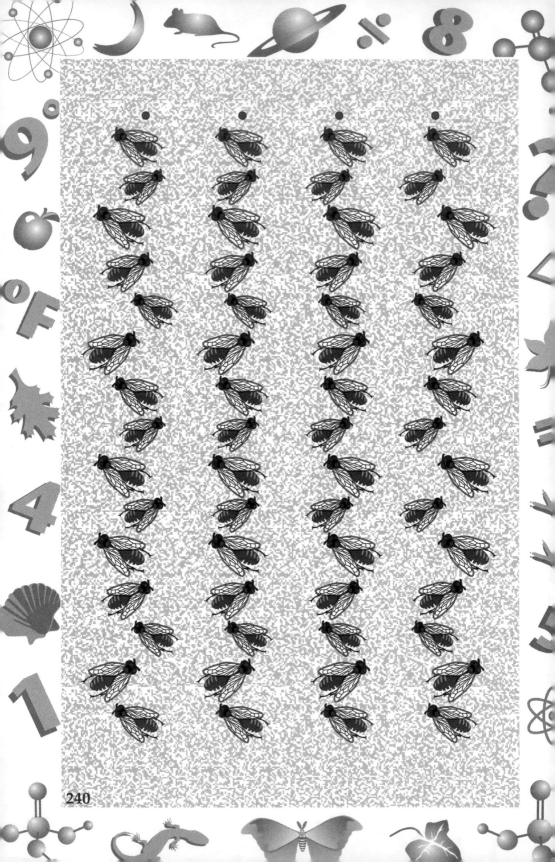

Dear Beakman,

How can you watch one TV channel while you videotape another channel? We even have cable and can't do it.

Glenn Peck
San Rafael,
California

Dear Glenn,

When you do something step by step, that is called a procedure (pro-SEE-duhr). Here is a procedure *You Can* use to see if your TV and VCR are hooked up right.

Beakman

Beakman Place

Why It Does Not Work
(Chart A)

Your cable box and your VCR and your TV all have tuners. A tuner is like a CHOOSER for channels. All the channels come into your house from the cable. The cable box will choose one channel only. Here it's the green channel.

Because your VCR is receiving just the green channel, the VCR's tuner (chooser) cannot choose another channel for you to watch while the VCR tapes the green channel. The cable box stopped the others because it can only choose one channel at a time.

You Can Make It Work Like This
(Chart B)

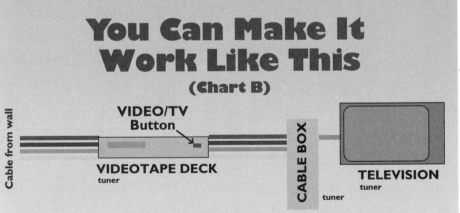

Your VCR can choose a channel to tape without stopping the other channels from going to your TV. The VCR's tuner chooses the channel it will tape. The VIDEO/TV switch lets YOU choose. You can choose to watch VIDEO (what the VCR's tuner has chosen) or you can choose TV - which is any other channel on your cable box.

You can watch one channel on the cable box's chooser while the VCR tapes a channel from its chooser. Your VCR must have a cable-ready tuner. If not, you can record only from cable channels 2 through 13. To watch a tape, select channel 3 or 4 on your cable box.

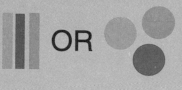

All the colors on your TV are made from just these three colors! Look real close and you can see them. Don't look too long. It is not good for your eyes!

VCR Procedure
Remember: Follow this step by step

1. Get a grown-up to help you. They will think they taught you something and that makes them feel good. Really you teach each other. But that is a secret. It is also safer to have a grown-up there and they bought the VCR so will want to be there. Get a grown-up!

2. Ask the grown-up to disconnect the power from the TV, the VCR and the cable box.

3. With your grown-up, follow the TV cable from the wall to see which comes first - the cable box or the VCR.

4. If your cable looks like Chart A the two of you have to change it to look like Chart B.

5. Grown-ups sometimes think things are harder to do than they really are. Stay there and help them by looking at the charts. Tell them you "know they can do it!"

6. When you get things all set up right, turn things on and try the VIDEO/TV switch. It lets YOU choose whether to watch the VCR's tuner or the cable box's tuner.

If you get any pay channels you will not be able to tape them. The cable box must choose pay channels. But you can watch a pay channel while you tape a free channel!

243

Dear Jax,

What are ghosts besides scary and gloomy?

Rachel Cameron
Waterloo,
Belgium

Dear Rachel,

Your terrific question shows us all that there are limits to what can be known and explained for sure.

Some things are either believed or not believed without any proof or reason. That's how it is with ghosts.

Maybe only humans can have or believe in ghosts because humans have something very special and wonderful - an imagination. Since we cannot prove anything about ghosts, let's talk about that - our imaginations - and what ghosts *might* be.

Jax Place

Jax Place

The Strength of Imagination

WHAT YOU NEED: Quiet time with yourself - pillow

WHAT TO DO: Lie down on your back somewhere that you like - a yard, a park or your room. Close your eyes and get peaceful-like. Decide to take yourself someplace else. *Notice everything* around you - the feel of the ground or your bed, the sounds, the temperature. Imagine you have all of those feelings in a new place. What would the new place be? What would you do there? What would it be like? Who are you in this new place?

WHAT IS GOING ON:
Talk about power! You just invented a whole new world all by yourself. Sometimes it's called a daydream, and daydreams are very important. They give your imagination room to stretch and grow. They give you ideas that you can't get anyplace else. They can help you solve problems of all kinds.

The next time someone tells you to stop daydreaming, you might tell them you're working on your imagination and it's working on you.

Ghosts – The Decision Is Yours

OK, so we know that *You Can* invent any reality you want with the powers of your imagination. Our imagination is certainly able to invent a few pretend ghosts to prowl around our rooms at night.

Still, many people say that the ghosts they've seen are *not* their imagination. Many others say ghosts do not exist at all. This makes things hard. The difficulty is deciding what is real without taking power away from your imagination. You don't want to make your imagination weak, because it's a very important thing.

Something that might help you decide is to help someone else. A friend or people in your family might get scared. They might tell you they've seen a ghost or a monster in their room. Tell them that it's terrific, fantastic and wonderful!

Ask them to show you and tell you all about it. *Don't ever* tell them, "It was *just* your imagination." Instead, tell them it's great that we can all see things in our own personal way. Sooner or later, the same thing will happen to you - you'll get scared. And then, you'll have to decide for yourself - was it a ghost, a personal vision, both or neither?

P.S. from Beakman: When we can't prove something but have some clues about it, we call that a theory (THEER-ee). Experiments are done to see if the clues are right. If an experiment doesn't work, we have to take a new look at things.

Dear Jax,

What is black pepper made of? Where does it come from?

Terry Dobyns
Streator, Illinois

Dear Terry,

Here's a little bet you can win with someone today. Black peppercorns come from: a. pepper trees; b. peppers; c. corn; d. vines; or e. shrubs?

When the early European explorers were out looking for a sailing route to the East, they were trying to find an easier way to get black pepper from Indonesia.

The bet is hard because we use the word *pepper* to describe lots of things - from cayenne to trees to jalapeño.

The correct answer is vines, up to 12 feet tall! They still grow in the Spice Islands of Southeast Asia.

Jax Place
Jax Place

Pepper Power

WHAT YOU NEED: Black pepper - bar of soap - toothpick - bowl of water

WHAT TO DO: Let the water get very, very still and quiet. Shake black pepper onto the water until the whole surface is covered with floating pepper.

Just touch the water with the toothpick. Be very gentle and still. Try not to disturb the pepper with the toothpick. Do the same thing with the corner of a bar of soap. Just touch it and pull it back. Compare what happened with the toothpick to what happened with the soap.

SO WHAT: OK, you got me. This has very little to do with what black pepper is made out of. It's just a fun thing to do with pepper.

The pepper sits on top of a kind of skin the water has, called the surface tension. The toothpick doesn't bother it. But the soap breaks that skin and the pepper jumps back as the skin breaks and jumps back.

The pepper jumps back from the soap in a split second!

Up Close & Personal

photo: Chloe Atkins

A microscope shows us that black pepper isn't really black. The berries are picked from the vine when they're green and then allowed to sit in the sun for a while. A black fungus called *Glomerella cingulata* grows on the skins. Yum! That's the only part that's black, the fungus. Green pepper is made by skipping the fungus-growing part. White pepper starts off as green pepper, but then the green skin is rubbed off.

P.S. from Beakman: The chemical in black pepper that makes us sneeze is called piperine (PIE-pur-een). It irritates our nose, and a sneeze is a kind of convulsion we have to clean it out.

Dear Stuart,

Sometimes the Moon seems to be absolutely enormous. It almost looks *delicious* when it's hanging there huge, right at the edge of the sky.

Compared to a tree or a house, the Moon is enormous. But compared to the vastness of the entire sky, the Moon is pretty small.

The difference is that comparison-thing. The difference is in your brain. And the moon only *seems* to be bigger or smaller because of what's available to compare it with.

Beakman

Beakman Place

Sizing It Up

WHAT YOU NEED: Night with a full moon - ruler

WHAT TO DO: Just as the Moon rises, hold the ruler out at the end of your arm. Reach all the way out as far as *You Can*. Close one eye and measure the Moon's width. Use your thumb as a guide. Wait a couple of hours until the Moon goes up into the night sky and measure it again.

Make sure you use the same arm and close the same eye both times.

SO WHAT: The Moon looked bigger when it was lower in the sky and smaller when it got higher. But it measured the same. That's because of how we judge things.

We put things in context. That means we look at everything that's near or beside each other. We see things *together*. When the Moon is together with the expanse of the entire sky, it seems smaller. Compared to the whole sky, it is.

When the Moon is high in the sky, it's pretty much all alone - a little dot in the big black bowl of the night.

Compared to What?

When the Moon is low in the sky, there are all kinds of things to compare it with - like trees, houses or the horizon line.

P.S. from Jax: Sometimes the Moon seems to be reddish or orange when it's near the horizon. That's because of all the air the moonlight has to go through. The air scattered out everything but the red or orange light waves, just like in a sunset.

Dear Jax,

How does a laser work?

Aaron Bielinski
Green Bay,
Wisconsin

Dear Aaron,

Lasers work because atoms get all excited and spit out light. All this excitement happens in between two mirrors that are a lot like those mirrored sunglasses Michael Jackson always wears.

We use laser light to play CDs, to scan those bar code things at the grocery store, and even to make phone calls. Laser light carries our calls through miles of thin strands of glass.

Jax Place
Jax Place

Fiber Optics at Home

WHAT YOU NEED: Small jar with lid - long black sock - flashlight - the kitchen sink - nail - hammer - darkness

WHAT TO DO: Punch 2 holes in the lid of the jar. Put the flashlight all the way into the bottom of the sock. Fill the jar with water and put on the lid. Slide the jar into the sock.

Turn off the lights. Turn on the flashlight. Now pour the water into your sink.

SO WHAT: Light travels in straight lines. That means your experiment should shine light along the line marked A. But it doesn't. Your light shone along line B. You just bent a beam of light around a corner. This is exactly how we can use laser light to send telephone calls down a long, curvy fiber of glass. Inside strands of glass and in streams of water, the light bounces off the inside walls. No matter which way the strand or stream bends, the light will follow it, bouncing along inside.

Tickle City

That's How a Laser Works

To understand lasers, you have to use your imagination. Imagine you're in a funhouse with your friends and you're all locked inside a bouncy rubber room. Now, one of you starts a tickling fight. The tickling grows until you're all doing it and you're all bouncing off the wall laughing like crazy. It gets so wild in there that you bust right out through one of the walls. That's sort of how a laser works, only it happens with atoms, and instead of laughter, they give off pure uniform light.

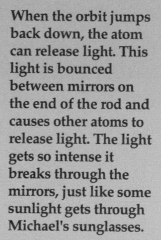

Light from a flash tube excites the atoms in a rod of ruby crystal. The orbit of the electrons can jump out.

When the orbit jumps back down, the atom can release light. This light is bounced between mirrors on the end of the rod and causes other atoms to release light. The light gets so intense it breaks through the mirrors, just like some sunlight gets through Michael's sunglasses.

P.S. from Beakman: Laser light is special because its light waves are in sync with each other. That means the light will not spread out like other light and can focus lots of energy tightly.